# IDENTIFYING SPECIAL NEEDS IN THE EARLY YEARS

**I**DENTIFYING SPECIAL NEEDS IN THE EARLY YEARS

Kay Mathieson

Paul Chapman Publishing

First published 2007

Paul Chapman Publishing
A SAGE Publications Company
1 Oliver's Yard
55 City Road
London EC1Y 1SP

SAGE Publications Inc.
2455 Teller Road
Thousand Oaks, California 91320

SAGE Publications India Pvt Ltd
B 1 I 1 Mohan Cooperative Industrial Area
Mathura Road, Post Bag 7
New Delhi 110 044

SAGE Publications Asia-Pacific Pte Ltd
33 Pekin Street #02-01
Far East Square
Singapore 048763

**Library of Congress Control Number: 2006936568**

A catalogue record for this book is available from the British Library

ISBN 978-1-4129-2906-6
ISBN 978-1-4129-2907-3 (pbk)

Typeset by Pantek Arts Ltd, Maidstone, Kent
Printed in Great Britain by The Cromwell Press, Trowbridge, Wilts.
Printed on paper from sustainable resources

# CONTENTS

# ACKNOWLEDGEMENTS

My thanks to Emma Hertzberg, Early Years Consultant (emma@hertzberg.co.uk), for the wonderful photographs which have made sure that the children's voices are heard in this book. I am indebted to the children, families and practitioners at the following settings for permission to use the photographs:

The Grove Nursery School, Peckham
Puddleduck Nursery, London SE22
Tatchbrook Nursery School, London SW1
Waverley School, Enfield
Rachel MacMillan Nursery School, Deptford

Putting together a book like this is inevitably a combination of ideas developed through working with many children, families and colleagues. Without everyone's contribution to the sharing and problem solving I have been part of over the years, this would have been a very short book. Thank you all.

Also thanks are due to Jude and the team at Paul Chapman Publishing. Without your encouragement I would never have started this journey.

Special thanks also to Simone. Yet again I couldn't have done it without your support!

# HOW TO USE THIS BOOK

The purpose of this book is to provide information and guidance about identifying and supporting children's additional needs in relation to their learning. The book can be used in a variety of ways depending on the situation and previous experience of the reader. It is arranged in eight chapters with an outline and summary of key points for each chapter. The intended audience for the book includes adults working in day nurseries, schools, pre-schools, nursery classes and toddler groups. The terminology used is a deliberate attempt to be inclusive; therefore, any adult working with children is referred to as a 'practitioner' and 'setting' is used to include all of these situations.

In terms of maximum impact on everyday practice, the ideal would be for the text and suggested good practice to be explored by a whole-staff group at the same time. But the experience of working through the suggestions in any group will increase confidence and enable individuals to influence the practice positively in their setting. For an individual, the book will provide reinforcement of good practice and prompts to reflect on current experience in any setting. The book can be used for reference, to dip into particular chapters as appropriate or to work through from beginning to end.

The suggested good practice can be used to facilitate group discussion and learning, or to prompt and develop personal reflection. The focus throughout the book is to identify and increase the frequency of observable good practice. The ultimate evidence of the understanding of the information contained in the chapters is that it informs the individual day-to-day practice of the practitioner. This cannot help but lead to improved experience for each child. This involves taking time to consider how we feel and what influences our reactions to specific situations. If this is done in a reflective and problem-solving way, it can lead to useful insight which can improve our practice. It does not, however, provide factual knowledge about what someone else is thinking or reasons for their actions. We must be prepared to amend our hypothesis in the light of further experience.

Ultimately, the book is a learning tool to be used flexibly to suit a particular situation. Remember that learning takes place best in relaxed and happy conditions, both for adults and for children, so I hope your experience of the book is also enjoyable!

# ABOUT THE AUTHOR

Kay Mathieson has taught in a variety of mainstream primary schools in both Scotland and England since 1981 when she qualified. In 1990 she began specialising in Special Educational Needs and has taught both infant and junior aged pupils with a variety of additional needs. Her interest in behaviour developed through her work in a Pupil Referral Unit and her experience in establishing an outreach support service to provide support before pupils were excluded.

She has delivered a range of INSET and training to staff groups, newly qualified teachers, support staff and Headteachers. She has been involved in writing *Better Behaviour in Classrooms* published by RoutledgeFalmer and *Social Skills in the Early Years, Supporting Behavioural Learning* published by Paul Chapman. From 2002 she was leading the Area SENCO team for Croydon Early Years Development and Childcare Partnership. In 2006 this role was extended to Inclusion Manager for the Early Education and Childcare Section of Croydon Education Department. She is also currently studying for a PhD at University of Sussex.

# Early identification

Working in partnership with parents is something which needs to be worked at and continually developed as a two-way relationship. Observation and assessment procedures can be used effectively to meet all children's needs. Using structured 'can do' statements can provide a positive starting point for realistic target setting. The adult role is crucial and needs to be planned for in as much detail as the next steps.

## What do we mean by early identification?

Early identification and early intervention for children with additional or special needs are talked about a lot these days, but I'm not sure we are always clear about what we mean by either phrase. In order to help all children make the most of their learning opportunities it is the role of the adults who care for them to look for ways to help make it easier for them to make sense of the world around them. In the first instance, at home parents care for, spend time with and provide interesting activities for children. These activities of talking to babies, showing them toys, tuning in to their needs, likes and dislikes are very important in supporting future learning. Parents are the adults who know individual children best and are their first educators. All children develop at different rates and in different ways. For example, we don't all walk or talk at the same age. However, generally speaking there are stages of development which roughly map out a child's progress in those early years. The Birth to Three Framework (Sure Start, 2002) gives good indications of the developmental progress of young children. All practitioners working in day nurseries and pre-schools will also have their training in child development to guide their view of children's development. As well as this general knowledge it is important that we use our knowledge of the individual child to identify progress and ways to help. One of the best ways to make sure that this view is accurate for each child we are working with is to share our evidence and thoughts with parents from day one of our involvement with the child. By working alongside parents from day one we gradually build up a picture together of the children as individuals and personalities. We can then plan together to use the children's developing interests and skills to help them explore and learn from the environment around them.

To enable this positive and proactive relationship with parents it is useful to review the information we provide for parents before their child joins us. Whatever we provide leads the parents to have expectations of what we can offer to them and their child as well as the way we will react to both them and their child. Sometimes it is helpful to decide as a staff group what impression you would like to make on parents during that first communication. Once you have agreed your priorities you can then improve your current information and contact with parents by focusing on how to communicate your priorities. Every opportunity you can find to get feedback from parents, both those who go on to place their child with you and those who decide not to, will help you to ensure that your setting is welcoming to your local community. Inviting parents into your setting for a variety of reasons and at a variety of times will help to keep you in touch with their views about your setting and support the continuation of positive relationships. It is such a powerful message for children to see their parents and caregivers from the setting working and communicating together in a positive way.

This establishment of an open, positive relationship with parents which is developed through mutual care and interest in the child is the most supportive context for a child's learning and development. In the context of this relationship it is possible to celebrate achievements, identify next steps for learning and share evidence of achievement. You may not always agree on every issue, but you have a context in which to have a professional and purposeful discussion with the mutual goal of the child's best interests at the centre of the relationship.

Good practice in early years settings is based on observation, assessment and planning for children's learning experiences. Good practitioners are able to evidence children's current learning and to link this evidence with planning for the child's next steps in learning. Clear systems are in place to document the observations for individual children and the ways in which their learning experiences are being supported. Sharing this information and talking through how and why decisions have been made ensures that parents have confidence in the practitioners caring for their child. It also helps to link opportunities for learning at home with current next steps in the setting. Sharing information about the child's responses to situations, new toys, relationships, etc. at home and at the setting can help parents and practitioners to celebrate and problem solve together as appropriate. In order to make this effective the routines in the setting need to be flexible enough to provide place and time for sharing information, ideas and concerns. Making such discussions a regular and frequent part of the child's and parents' experience of your setting helps to confirm confidence in the fact that everyone is working together for the child's best interests and that even if things are not going as smoothly as we would like, we can work together to suggest and try different ways to help.

As information about the child's achievements and development builds up, a pattern will begin to emerge about the personality and likes and dislikes the child has in a variety of contexts. This will build from special toys, music, ways of being cuddled as a baby through to ways in which the child communicates their needs and wants. Finding out about the child's communication and being able to identify their needs quickly and effectively will help to ensure that the child will feel secure and relaxed with you. Checking out this information and sharing this knowledge and understanding with colleagues makes sure that everyone has the opportunity to respond consistently and supportively to the child even if their keyworker is not present.

**Which of your children prefer to learn outside?**

From this bank of knowledge and information, the adults involved will begin to predict how children will react in certain situations. They will develop shared expectations of what children will like as an activity, preferred ways of communicating if they don't want something and who they will like to be with at a particular time.

There is sometimes a feeling that if we don't voice our concern about a child's progress, then we won't need to do anything about it; if it is that important, someone else will do something about it. This view usually comes from either uncertainty about what to do or fear and anxiety about the reaction we may get from parents. The easiest ways to counteract these barriers are to have frequent conversations with colleagues about different concerns which are identified, clarify the procedures in the setting which need to be followed if you have a concern, and most importantly to attend local training. By attending local training as an individual you will become more confident and knowledgeable about the local support and advice which is available and how this support can be accessed.

The fear and anxiety which is experienced by practitioners with regards to talking to parents about concerns relating to children's progress can be broken down on an individual and setting level. On an individual level it is a significant part of our role in caring for children to establish and maintain positive relationships with all parents. Inevitably there will be some parents with whom we find this easier than with others but by taking on the professional role of working in childcare we must accept the responsibility to take the lead in the relationship with parents, for the benefit of the children in our care. The characteristics of this relationship are crucial and need to be regularly reviewed with opportunity for feedback from parents about ways in which we can improve. To be effective the relationship needs to be based on professional priorities. Being friends might make things easier on a day-to-day basis but can mean that we find it harder to initiate more difficult conversations. The relationship needs to be explicitly two way: parents can bring concerns to us as well as us sharing concerns with them. The ideal is to have clear opportunities for extended discussion in an appropriate place, with the professional setting the tone of a joint problem-solving approach to the discussion. Basic things which can help to build this context and relationships with parents are to:

- ask current parents for feedback about their first experiences of the setting

- ask for suggestions of ways to make the setting information more accessible

- check that the first contacts with parents invite further discussion and involvement

- check through the year's events in the setting calendar and have parents and families identify ways in which they could be more involved

- discuss with staff concerns and anxieties about talking to parents, identifying ways in which these can be addressed either through training, mentoring or changes in setting practice

- identify what you consider to be good practice in relationships with parents and families, sharing this with parents and asking for feedback and suggestions about ways to improve and make the experience more consistent

- review the ways in which building positive relationships with parents is included in your induction for new members of the staff team

- review as a staff team everyone's expectations of individual responsibilities in working in partnership with parents and families.

The starting point for some of these discussions with staff could be to consider that every relationship with parents and families should begin with the expectation that at some point in the future there will be a need for a difficult conversation. If we start out thinking everything is always going to go smoothly, we often begin to make assumptions about how others think which are based on very little real information. These assumptions then become a reason for not keeping parents involved, for example thinking parents don't have time to talk, don't want to talk, don't spend enough time with their children, don't know enough about their children, have an unrealistic view of their children. These assumptions are often 'don't' or 'can't' phrases and tend to be statements which enhance our own role by implication: where parents can't or don't we think we can and do. If these assumptions begin to characterise discussion in the setting about parents generally or individually, this is a danger sign that our relationships are not being maintained in an effective way. Trying to see things from a parent's perspective can be very difficult if our personal experience is quite different from the parent concerned. However, there are some key ideas which may help:

- Parents want the best for their children.

- It is a difficult decision to choose a childcare setting which is convenient, affordable and somewhere you feel able to leave your child.

- Parents are likely to experience feelings of guilt and a sense of missing out on elements of their child's development.

■ In the current climate parents will have concerns and doubts about what their child is doing and the quality of the care being provided for their child.

It is inevitable that at first you and the parent will be talking about a different child. It is impossible for the parent to see their child in a group situation with 'new' adults without being present. The child is having to learn about and cope with a huge range of new situations and relationships which you will observe but the parent is unable to see directly. Parents are the best advertising for your setting so it is worth your investment in ensuring that they are involved in the development of your policies and procedures. Needless to say, having established these policies and procedures, they then need to be implemented effectively and reviewed with staff and parents regularly.

Developing a quality learning environment for all children will be based on a variety of elements, including our knowledge of:

■ child development

■ Birth to Three Matters, the Foundation Stage Curriculum and associated guidance

■ providing quality learning opportunities

■ the role of the adult in supporting children's learning

■ relationships between the children in the group.

**With adult help**

**On my own!**

There are several ways in which we establish and build on each of these elements. Our initial training should provide the basis for our future learning about our role in the lives of the children for whom we provide care. Anyone who considers that completing minimum qualifications to get a job in childcare is sufficient to maintain an effective and satisfying career needs to think carefully about their motivation and professionalism. Through training we learn about using observation to evidence children's current learning and what we need to provide to identify and help them achieve next steps. The quality of these observations is crucial to the effective identification of children's learning. These observations form the basis of our shared knowledge of the children's progress with their parents. Being clear about the next steps for a child's learning gives us the opportunity to involve parents and families in their children's learning experiences. In turn, this gives us the chance to have ongoing discussions about a child's rate of progress which is often one of the first indicators of concern surrounding a child's particular needs.

There are many sources of support and information about observation and planning effectively. First, the principles of good practice at the beginning of the Foundation Stage Curriculum (DfES/QCA, 2000, pp. 11–31) set the context. Secondly, *Seeing Steps in Children's Learning* (QCA, 2005a) and *Observing Children – Building the Profile* (QCA, 2005b) give examples of observations, ways to support children's learning and possible next steps. There are also several books available which work through the issues related to both observation and assessment and the essential links between them.

For our purposes the key elements are that our observations are done frequently and regularly, have sufficient detail to make assessments and are recorded in a positive way.

Over time our observations should have representation of a variety of learning situations, including:

- child-initiated play

- group play

- group activities

- practitioner-led activities

- planned activities which are set up for children to experience and carry out independently.

(*Observing Children – Building the Profile*, QCA, 2005b)

They should also cover the range of curriculum areas. Whatever the format of observation, they can be effectively enhanced with the addition of photographic evidence which is dated and annotated. This also provides a very effective way of involving parents in their children's experience of the setting.

Through our collection of observations and planning for next steps in children's learning we gradually build a picture of the child's individual learning pattern, likes, dislikes, strengths and learning needs. This information is then available for us to use to inform what adults need to do to support the child in a variety of ways and situations. By looking collectively at the evidence for all the children in the group, we can begin to evaluate the effectiveness of the learning environment we are offering. The activities we offer should be clearly indicated through our observations and next steps; therefore if children's learning does not seem to be progressing effectively, we should firstly consider the learning activities we are providing. Equally, the impact of the adult role cannot be underestimated. Over the past twenty years there has been a significant shift in our understanding of the importance of the role of the adult in a child's learning. This could perhaps be described as a move from a passive 'delivery of activity' role to a proactive 'companion in learning' role. This is also mirrored in some of the ways in which society generally has changed in the collective thinking about what is best for children. We no longer expect that children should be seen and not heard but neither is there acceptance that children should be able to do exactly as they please. As childcare workers we need to be clear about our expectations of children and our justification in current guidance for these principles. From these principles the expectations of the role of the adults in the setting will be established. As individuals we often have some difficulty in translating the knowledge we gain through training, reading and experience to what we actually have to do and say when we are with the children. Again this is a topic which can very usefully be used for discussion at staff meetings, during appraisals and as part of the induction process. The more opportunity there is for us to clarify our understanding of the role we can play in children's learning, the more confident we will feel in approaching our interactions with individual children. This is particularly true where there is a focus on an agreement about what good practice would look like in a particular situation.

Within this context of working in partnership with families and explicitly identifying good practice, we have the best possible chance of recognising when we have a concern about a child's progress. We are therefore in a position to be able to have a positive discussion with parents and to plan effectively for the child's learning.

## What do we mean by early intervention?

Practitioners often feel that they need to do something very different or special for particular children. This is seldom the case if a view of the child's needs are seen in the context of their learning in all areas.

Observation and planned, supported learning opportunities are part of current practice for all children. Once we have identified a concern through our usual observation process and discussed this with parents, our next step is likely to be more focused observation in order to gather further detail of our concern. With this further level of detail we can then construct a selection of 'can do' statements which clearly identify the child's current level of achievement in this context. There is much talk about getting the balance between being 'too positive' about a child's abilities and not clearly communicating areas of difficulty. I would argue that if the following structure for 'can do' statements is used, a practitioner should be able to see not only that there is a need for support but also the extent of the need. The structure I would suggest has the following three elements:

1 description of observable behaviour

2 context in which behaviour occurs

3 length of time the behaviour continues for.

These elements then fit into a clear statement as follows:

*Ebony can share a picture book with an adult in the book corner for five minutes.*

Having focused on the detail of our observations we now need to look for the adult role in moving Ebony's learning forward. If our ultimate aim is to help Ebony to be part of a group story-time, we need to think about what our first step on the way might be. From our 'can do' statement we know that Ebony can share a book with an adult for five minutes. To change this to a target we need to decide which of the three elements we will change. We could change the context to either sharing a book with an adult and a child or extend the time from five minutes to seven or eight minutes. We would not decide to change more than one element at a time. Our target could, for example, become:

*Ebony will share a picture book with an adult and one other child in the book corner for five minutes.*

Setting a target does not, however, change a child's behaviour but it should change the adult's behaviour. Having decided on the appropriate target our next task is to identify what we can do to give Ebony the best possible chance of achieving this next step. These can often be covered with the following four 'Ps':

- Practise – the opportunity to practise some of the elements which will be needed to achieve the target, for example highlighting times when Ebony sits with an adult and one other child involved in any activity.

- Prepare – reflect on previous success and what made it successful.

■ Prompt – use particular phrases, gestures, signs which help Ebony to approach the situation with the best possible chance of success.

■ Praise – use the form and level of praise which is most effective for Ebony.

This process can be used for any next step for learning, including behavioural learning which we often find most challenging to think about. As a process it also consolidates the positive relationship with parents and focuses on the current achievements of the child.

 **Key points**

■ Partnership with parents provides a foundation for positively supporting all children's learning.

■ Staff teams need to clarify their ideas of good practice which are used in training, appraisal and induction processes.

■ In developing relationships with parents staff need to be clear about their responsibilities and the roles of other team members such as the Special Educational Needs Co-ordinator (SENCO), Room Leader, Deputy Manager, Manager.

■ Using a structured 'can do' statement can help to communicate clearly progress children are making and what could be worked on next.

## Suggestions for learning about children with their parents

The usual initial information, such as name, address, contact details, emergency contact, ethnicity, dietary requirements and medical information, is fairly standard in admission procedures for all settings these days but it is useful to review how the information is collected. Ideally the first gathering of information will set the tone of the future relationship with parents by taking place in a conversational context rather than a pure question and answer session. By phrasing questions carefully those involved are able to expand on the basic answer.

**What other information might we want?**
**How would you phrase the question to make it conversational?**

■ What situations do you think your child will really enjoy about being at this nursery?

■ How do you think your child will show their enjoyment of situations?

■ How would you like us to let you know about these enjoyable times?

■ What situations do you think your child will find more difficult about being at this nursery?

▶

- How do you think your child will show their anxiety or distress?

- What do you do at home when your child feels this way?

- Compare with the way practitioners in the setting would respond and talk about any differences.

- In what ways does your child communicate that they are hungry, thirsty, tired, needing the toilet?

- What is your child's usual experiences of meal times – eating alone, with one other, whole family together; sitting at a table, on the floor, watching television, talking, etc. Compare with the routine in the setting and explain how you will help the child to learn about the new expectations.

- What is your child's experience of nappy changing, toileting? Are there any special routines which could be used in the setting, e.g. particular songs, particular phrases which are used, order in which things are done, ways in which the child can be involved in the process such as collecting the wipes/cream, etc.?

- How does your child respond at the moment if they are asked to let another child play with the same toy/game? Which things does your child find easiest to share, most difficult to share?

These sorts of questions lead to more of a discussion and a finding out about the child, as an individual. The information gathered can then form the basis of a respectful relationship with the child, taking an interest in their needs, likes and dislikes. The first few days of a relationship between a child and their keyworker and the family and keyworker can be considerably enhanced if the child recognises similarities between home and the setting. It will also reduce the anxiety of both parents and practitioners in those early discussions so making the 'settling period' for the child easier.

It is also really helpful to review with parents what their feelings were about your initial procedures after the child has been with you for a couple of months.

The photocopiable sheets that follow provide a summary of key points covered in the chapter. These can be used as handouts to help practitioners review the aims, ideas and any action which has been discussed or agreed.

'Can do' statements can give a clear indication of a child's current achievements and provide the basis for identifying next steps.

To be effective the 'can do' statement has to have three key elements:

1 description of observable behaviour

2 context in which behaviour occurs

3 length of time the behaviour continues for.

Our target could, for example, become:

*Ebony will share a picture book with an adult and one other child in the book corner for five minutes.*

Once the 'can do' statement has been identified it is important to be specific about what the adults will do to enable children to achieve the next step.

## The four 'Ps'

The four 'Ps' give a clear structure to help clarify what the adults need to do. Thinking about the example of Ebony:

- **Practise** — the opportunity to practise some of the elements which will be needed to achieve the target, for example highlighting times when Ebony sits with an adult and one other child involved in any activity.

- **Prepare** — reflect on previous success and what made it successful.

- **Prompt** — use particular phrases, gestures, signs which help Ebony to approach the situation with the best possible chance of success.

- **Praise** — use the form and level of praise which is most effective for Ebony.

# CHAPTER 2

# Child development

Key ideas and theories can be identified which have influenced our current practice in supporting children's learning. Finding ways to ensure that significant information is shared effectively with colleagues to support children's development is an important first step. It can be particularly helpful to think about behavioural learning in the same way as other areas of the curriculum. The observation, assessment and planning cycle can effectively support children's individual learning needs.

For centuries people have been fascinated by the way in which children learn and develop. The vast amount of learning which takes place from birth to five years old is amazing. It has been a constant focus of research to try to find out more detail about how children mange to learn so much in such a short space of time to such a high level of mastery. This process of research has many strands, including:

- Function of different areas of the brain.

- Complexities of language which need to be mastered.

- General communication and relationships.

- Identifying how learning takes place.

- Finding ways of providing optimum learning opportunities for young children.

Initially, researchers used observation of their own children to inform their developing theories. Often, assessment tasks presented for children relied on a verbal response which limited the age at which effective responses could be gathered. This is one of the key criticisms of some of Piaget's work and some of the assessments have been revisited, offering the possibility of a non-verbal response. This has extended our understanding of how early some children are able to achieve certain conceptual knowledge. Communication is a very complex area to investigate and is now supported by ever-increasing technology to monitor and identify the communication process. Increasingly, we are able to gather more detailed information which confirms that babies take an active part in the communication process long before speech develops. This also has a significant impact on the importance of early relationships and the evident need for a baby to have significant, consistent adults to develop close, secure and nurturing relationships. If these first relationships are positive and attuned with the child's needs, then they provide a foundation from which children are able to explore further with confidence. They are secure in the knowledge that, should the need arise, they can retreat to their first attachments to feel safe again.

The main vehicle for young children's learning is undoubtedly play. The importance of providing appropriate opportunities for exploring ideas, concepts, relationships and skills through play cannot be over-stated. Several researchers have examined and observed the function of play in a child's development. Increasingly, it is acknowledged that being able to try things out, 'play' with ideas, try being different people, get things wrong are essential elements of valuable play which need to be supported and valued by sensitive adults.

Table 2.1 gives a brief summary of some of the key theorists who have significantly influenced our views of children's development. Most of these theorists have been involved in a broad range of research. The key ideas listed are just those for which they are best known in the field of child development.

These theorists all impact on our daily work with children. We may not consciously think of their names as we work but their research has influenced current approaches to childcare. It is important to understand the role which these theories play in our own responses to the children we support. Currently there is no 'right answer' about how children learn or what they bring to the learning activities. However, the research which builds on the work of these theorists increasingly refines the evidence of how children learn and develop. As each year passes more complex technology is available to aid research and analyse results to give us more detailed information. Child development and theories of learning are topics which need to be revisited regularly during our careers in childcare. We can do this through training courses, our own reading and sharing new ideas during staff meetings. Most early years journals such as *Nursery World*, *Early Years Educator* and *Preschool Practice* have reference to new research and its impact. They also highlight and review new books which will support questioning and improving our own practice. The process of implementing the ideas raised in research within our day-to-day practice has to involve discussion and critical thinking with our colleagues. Thinking through what good practice would look like in our own setting in light of the different approaches is part of developing our professional approach to childcare.

**Watching**

**Copying**

The Early Years Foundation Stage (0–5) document (DfES, 2006) builds on recent research and theories concerning child development and learning. Developmental stages are identified as:

Birth to 11 months

8–20 months

16–26 months

22–36 months

30–50 months

40–60$^+$ months.

The document clearly makes the point that although there can be some general guidance about what children may be able to accomplish at each stage, this is by no means a rigid checklist. The stages are deliberately overlapping to underline the fact that developmental progress is different for each child. Children all develop and acquire skills, abilities and knowledge at different times and the focus must be to use observation of individual children to plan for their progress.

*It is important that practitioners ensure that they observe closely what children can do, and use those observations as the basis of assessment and planning of the next stages of children's development.* (DfES, 2006, p. 8)

The Early Years Foundation Stage document is designed to be inclusive and the broad age ranges of the developmental stages are in keeping with inclusive thinking. The focus on individual needs and progress is a positive approach for all children. However, we also need to consider what might be the triggers for our concerns to be raised about a particular child's progress and the need to seek further advice.

**Table 2.1  Key theorists and their ideas in the field of child development**

| Theorist | Key ideas | Dates |
|---|---|---|
| Ivan Pavlov | Researched conditioning responses to specific stimulus | 1849–1936 |
| Sigmund Freud | Psychoanalysis and the impact of early experiences on later learning, development and understanding. Suggested stages in psychosexual development. He argued that experiences through these early stages impact on later feelings about self and relationships with others | 1856–1939 |
| Susan Isaacs | Play essential as vehicle for children's learning and healthy mental development. Importance of parents being involved in children's learning experiences | 1885–1948 |
| Jean Piaget | Cognitive Development Theory. Stages of development, understanding of concepts | 1896–1980 |
| Donald Winnicott | Play important for children to use imaginative experience to work out anxieties and new experiences | 1896–1971 |
| Lev Vygotsky | Development of ideas about internal and external function of language. Identified concept of the Zone of Proximal Development to indicate the potential of a child's learning rather than only considering retrospectively the learning which has taken place. Raised the status and importance of play as a vehicle for children's learning | 1896–1934 |
| Erik Erikson | Followed Freud's work to focus on developing 'healthy personalities' and achieving a 'unified self' | 1902–1994 |
| Burrhus Frederic Skinner | Developed ideas about conditioning and the role of positive and negative reinforcement in increasing occurrence of particular behaviours | 1904–1990 |
| John Bowlby | Attachment theory and the importance of early bonding experience with main carer | 1907–1990 |
| Jerome Bruner | Children's three systems of learning: using action to manipulate objects; employing sensory-based mental images; symbolic representation through language and reasoning | 1915– |
| Urie Bronfenbrenner | Identified the importance of the interaction between the different communities which the child experiences For example, family, extended family, childcare setting, religious community, local community, etc | 1917–2005 |
| Albert Bandura | Social learning theory; children learn from role models around them | 1925– |
| Noam Chomsky | Children born with innate ability to develop language which comes 'on line' as child matures | 1928– |
| Chris Athey | Developed the idea of schemas, which link repeated actions with increasing complexity of learning, such as enveloping things, joining things, etc. Schemas gradually become interlinked as they develop | |
| Colwyn Trevarthen | Focuses on communication initiated by babies from minutes after birth. Explores the musicality of language and responses of babies to reciprocal communication with main carer | |
| Margaret Donaldson | The need for the impact of appropriate, everyday experiences to support learning | |
| Ferre Laevers | Deeper-level learning takes place if highly involved in activity. Focused on measuring learning taking place using scale showing levels of involvement in task. Linked to this raised profile of role of the adult through development of engagement scales | |

*Source*: Based on *Birth to Three Matters* (Sure Start, 2002, Literature review, ch. 2)

The information and experience we gain, through observation, enables us in discussion with our colleagues to ensure realistic expectations of children's developments. If we have realistic expectations of what children of a particular age, stage, ability and personality might achieve, this would also give us an awareness of what would cause concern. Getting the balance between our knowledge of child development and when particular milestones are likely to be reached and when to be concerned, is something which worries all adults at some time. Clearly not all two-year-olds are able to do the same things to the same level of competency. Therefore any judgements we make must also take into account our knowledge of the child's ability in other areas of learning, their personality and the opportunities for learning which the child has experienced. Our knowledge of individual children should not be solely from our own experience but should be a collective understanding involving the professional views of our colleagues who will see the child from a slightly different perspective. The discussions we have with parents need to be central to any judgements we may make about children's progress. Keeping parents involved in their children's learning is crucial if we are to include them in our decision making about appropriate next steps and priorities. It gives a much richer and more informed picture of the child's development if we are able to take account of progress at home as well as in the setting. It is important to recognise that children will show the best of their skills and knowledge when they are most relaxed and this will often be in their own home.

In the context of this relationship with parents, it is possible to share understanding of our increasing knowledge of the child's learning style and pace. We can share with parents the observations which inform our next steps and agree with parents the best way for us to support the child to achieve them. Through giving frequent and regular updates on the child's response to our attempts we can create a culture of joint problem solving with the parents. This enables us to share surprises about things the child learnt quicker than expected as well as things that have taken longer to master. By involving parents from the observation stage we can take them on a journey with us which focuses on their child's development. When progress is not as we expect the conversation is supported by observational evidence and we are able to involve parents in deciding what needs to happen next. As we develop a picture of the normal pattern of learning for an individual child, we then have an opportunity to consider if further help or advice would be helpful. In the first instance this would be about sharing concerns with the setting SENCO and colleagues who have knowledge of the child. This process of seeking further advice needs to be discussed sensitively with parents and they should be involved as much as possible in the process. Ideally, they would join the discussion between keyworker and SENCO to review the observations, discuss the concerns and decide on the next course of action. Where this process of joint decision making is central to the culture of a setting, parents will feel more confident and less anxious about involving professionals from outside the setting, such as the Area SENCO Team, inclusion support teams, etc.

The process of discussing children's progress with colleagues needs to be given an appropriate professional context. This discussion will be based on evidence from observations, progress towards next steps, adult role in supporting learning and its impact. It will involve colleagues asking searching questions about what else the adult might do, activities which might provide better opportunity for learning and the child's responses to other situations. These conversations are important on several levels, including between:

- the room team

- keyworker and room leader

- SENCO and keyworker

- SENCO and room leader

- SENCO and member of management team.

We each have a responsibility to make these discussions useful and focused on supporting the child's progress in a positive way. It is all too easy to follow someone's negative comments with more of our own but this has no place in making professional decisions.

> *Practitioners must ensure that the individual needs of all children are met, including additional or different provision required to meet particular individual needs.* (DfES, 2006, p. 13)

Our focus is to find ways to bring together our knowledge, experience and information in a meaningful way which can be part of problem-solving discussions. Using our observation and assessment practice we can focus on positive approaches to children's learning in all areas of development. This should specifically include social and emotional aspects of learning.

When we talk about all areas of learning we often overlook behavioural learning as an area of the curriculum. Somehow we see behavioural learning as something which children should simply acquire or just know without us planning for or supporting the learning. I would suggest that if we think about behavioural learning in the same way as other areas of the curriculum, we can apply the same approaches to helping children learn. By using our observations, assessments and 'can do' statements we can plan for and support children to develop their social behavioural competency. This is a situation which highlights the importance of the adult role being one of learning companion and seeing the situation from the child's perspective. Behavioural learning is something which adults find one of the most challenging issues related to inclusion and meeting children's needs. Seeing social, emotional and behavioural learning in the same way as other areas of learning enables us to use our skills and experience to provide positive learning opportunities. This includes finding ways of involving children in making choices and having a voice about what help they need and how it is offered. The idea of taking account of children's views and choices can be challenging to think through at first sight, particularly for very young children. However, once we know children well enough to be able to understand how they communicate, when they are happy or unhappy, then we are able to take account of their choices. It does not matter how these emotions are communicated to us; it is part of our role to be able to interpret and tune in to these communications.

## How does this fit with what we already do?

There have been significant changes in provision for young children in recent years and practitioners have been the focus of government and media attention for some time. This focus has resulted in much imposed change but also considerable questioning of everyday practice. For the private and voluntary sectors there has also been a shift from purely inspection to a combination of support and inspection. The current situation is that the majority of early years practitioners have access to advice, training and professional development with colleagues.

**Playing alongside**

With this increased access to knowledge and expertise comes a clearer focus on the variety of ways in which we can support young children's development. Seeing ourselves as having a significant role as learning companions for young children requires that we find effective ways to document and plan to provide support for each individual child. Part of this process is to record observations, assessment and planning in sufficient detail to communicate to ourselves, colleagues, parents and other involved professionals. This recording is about focusing our efforts to increase our knowledge of the individual child and to use this knowledge to provide opportunities and experiences which can be used to maximise children's learning. The same is true for any child whether or not they are identified as having an additional need. Every child will, at times, need particular help to overcome the challenges of a new piece of learning. With parents and our colleagues we can identify the bridge from previous learning which will make the new learning accessible.

## Key points

- Our current practice is based on specific theories and research about children's learning and development. The Early Years Foundation Stage document identifies broad developmental age bands as guidance, not as a rigid checklist.

- We need to revise our knowledge of theories and current research regularly through our career.

- Communication between colleagues is influential in establishing realistic and consistent expectations of individual children.

- We can work with parents to find ways to ensure that children's views are taken into account and inform our strategies.

- It is important to identify the specific adult role in supporting children's achievement of their next steps.

- Seeing behavioural learning in the same way as other areas of the curriculum can be a more effective way of supporting children's learning.

- It is the adult's role to interpret the child's communication, be it verbal or behavioural.

- We all need help at sometime in our learning. Good practice for children with additional needs is good practice for all children.

There are many suggested formats which can be used for observation and it is important that as a staff group you review your existing format regularly to ensure that it continues to meet your needs and is easily shared with parents. The 'Observation framework' photocopiable is a suggested framework which can be used to support observations.

Time, date, place and context of the observation need to be noted as well as the name of the person observing and, if appropriate, the purpose of the observation.

Things to look for:

- Level of involvement in the activity (this could be guided by the Leuven Scales developed by Ferre Laevers).

- Length of time the child remains at the activity.

- Did the child choose the activity independently?

- How many children were there when the child approached?

- What is the child's response when another child joins the activity?

- In what way does the child interact/join in with the other children?

- In what way does the child respond to any adults near by?

- What is the child able to do physically with the equipment?

- In what way does the child display use of their imagination during play?

- Are there any signs of frustration in the child's behaviour? If so, what skill/knowledge would help to reduce the frustration?

- Which of the child's interests could be used to develop the activity and extend the child's learning?

Again date, time, place, observer need to be noted.

The purpose of observation would probably link to a previous, more general observation or comment from parent or practitioner. It is particularly important that the purpose of the observation is not taken to prove our assumptions correct but to accurately collect information around a particular situation.

■ Record accurate timing of the focus response (e.g. flitting).

■ Look for times when the focus response does not happen — these exceptions are often the key to how we can help.

■ Identify things which change, prevent or increase the focus response (e.g. what helps to engage the child's interest for longest even if this is only one minute?).

■ Look for key relationships or interactions, either with adults or children, which change the child's response.

■ Look for specific triggers which lead to the focus response (e.g. no response from others at the activity, another child playing alongside).

Compare focus observations made at different times of day and in different contexts — for example, inside and outside learning environments.

The frequency of observations will depend on the purpose or focus. As well as regular short observations to monitor children's general progress it is useful to use them to follow up or clarify things. This clarification may be needed to gather more information about something surprising which has been commented on, such as a child being able to sustain relationships with a group of children when involved in a particular activity. Alternatively, there may be a general feeling that a child is flitting from one activity to another rather than getting involved in purposeful play. To begin with, this may just be a feeling without real evidence and we can often over- or underestimate the real frequency or extent of this behaviour. Through exploring further using targeted observation, perhaps at particular times of day, we can build a picture of what is really happening for the child (see the 'Targeted observation' photocopiable). Once we have the evidence it is much easier to decide if we need to do something and what that something might be.

Observation notes should always be written with the expectation that they will be shared with parents, professionals and colleagues. They should be factual descriptions of what is seen with no judgemental phrases or words such as 'he only stayed for two minutes', 'she just put two bricks together', etc.

Once the observation has been carried out the evidence can be shared with colleagues and parents and talked through with suggestions about what the next step of learning might be. Further information can be gained from comparing observations over time: looking back at the observations made over the past couple of months can show clear progress, changes in interest or sustained difficulty with a particular skill or area of knowledge.

It is often helpful to have discussions with the whole-staff group about particular scenarios and whether or not they would cause us to be concerned. The discussion can help to identify what impacts on our thinking and decision making. The final two photocopiables of the chapter can be used to start your discussions off before moving on to children who are attending your setting.

Think about what you know about the child's current learning pattern. Check your observations to provide evidence for your answers.

■ How quickly does the child usually learn a new skill?

■ What helps the child to learn effectively – watching others, copying, practising themselves, working with a friend, etc.?

■ In relation to other children of a similar age and stage, is the child's response unusual?

■ Do all the adults who know the child have a similar view about their progress – if not, what would help to clarify things more?

■ Is the child's learning pattern similar in all areas?

■ What are the child's particular strengths?

## Scenario 1

A child runs round the room briefly touching a variety of equipment and shouting

## Things to think about (for all scenarios)

Would you be concerned if the child was:
10 months    1 year    2 years    3 years    4 years

Would you be concerned if the child did this:
Once   Once a day   Twice a day   10 times a day   20 times a day

Would you be concerned if the child did this for:
2 minutes    5 minutes    10 minutes    30 minutes    50 minutes

## Scenario 1: If you were concerned, what would you do?

Use focused observation to find out:

- what might be the trigger for the behaviour?

- what is the child's motivation for the behaviour, e.g. what activities are involved?

- when is the child least likely to respond in this way?

- when is the child most likely to respond in this way?

- what response does the child get from other adults and children?

From this factual information you can then decide how the adults will respond to the behaviour, for example:

- ignore and praise the children walking or involved in activity

- meet the child and take them for a walk round the room to see what is available

- set up activities which are particularly motivating for the child and support any initial engagement in the activity

- reduce the choice on offer for the child in the first instance, e.g. 'you can choose the building or painting first today'.

## Scenario 2

A child frequently chooses painting activities at the easel, often dropping the paintbrush and making a mess on the floor

## Scenario 2: If you were concerned, what would you do?

Use focused observation to find out:

- what might be the trigger for the behaviour — is it deliberate or accidental?
- what is the child's motivation for the behaviour, e.g. to gain attention?
- when is the child least likely to respond in this way?
- when is the child most likely to respond in this way?
- what response does the child get from other adults and children?

## Scenario 3

When playing outside the child runs up to other children and hits them

## Scenario 3: If you were concerned, what would you do?

Use focused observation to find out:

- what might be the trigger for the behaviour?
- what is the child's motivation for the behaviour, e.g. to make contact with the children?
- when is the child least likely to respond in this way?
- when is the child most likely to respond in this way?
- what response does the child get from other adults and children?

## Scenario 4

When given instructions by an adult the child looks blank and carries on playing

## Scenario 4: If you were concerned, what would you do?

Use focused observation to find out:

- what might be the trigger for the behaviour — can the child hear you?
- what is the child's motivation for the behaviour, e.g. to carry on with a favourite activity?
- when is the child least likely to respond in this way?
- when is the child most likely to respond in this way?
- what response does the child get from other adults and children?

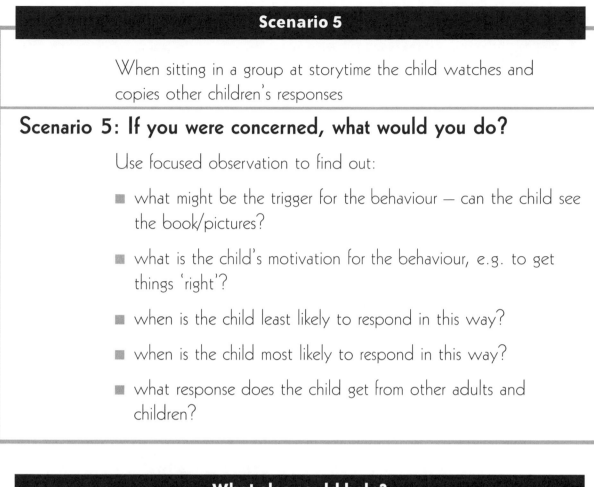

## Scenario 5

When sitting in a group at storytime the child watches and copies other children's responses

## Scenario 5: If you were concerned, what would you do?

Use focused observation to find out:

- what might be the trigger for the behaviour — can the child see the book/pictures?

- what is the child's motivation for the behaviour, e.g. to get things 'right'?

- when is the child least likely to respond in this way?

- when is the child most likely to respond in this way?

- what response does the child get from other adults and children?

## What else could help?

From the evidence gathered through your observations you have a good basis for a discussion with other adults who know the child and other professionals who may be able to help you.

- Talk to colleagues including the SENCO to check out your ideas and the extent of your concern.

- Talk to the parents about what you have observed and what you intend to do about it; ask if they have noticed similar things. If not, it might be different because of the number of children in the group, the size of the room, the length of time the child has been attending the setting, etc.

- Ask parents if they would be happy for you to talk to the Health Visitor or inclusion support teams for advice. Invite them to be there too.

CHAPTER 3

# Sharing the learning journey with parents

For some parents leaving their child in the care of others in an unfamiliar building can be a very anxious experience. There are many valid reasons why parents may be particularly anxious about their child. It is our role as practitioners to initiate and maintain positive relationships with all parents. Our observations provide evidence of children's experience and form a basis for discussion about planning for the child's learning. Parents' observations and knowledge about their child provide crucial insights into the ways in which we can best help them.

**Parents and practitioners both learn about the child they share.**

When parents bring their children to our setting they bring a collection of preconceived ideas of what the childcare experience may be like for their child. These meet our preconceived ideas about what parenting experiences their child may have had. Current parents have not generally experienced the same levels of childcare as their children. Combine this with the variety of media coverage, both good and bad, which our day nurseries and pre-schools have had and it is not surprising that there are some misunderstandings. It is our role as practitioners to work for the best interests of the children in our care. In order to do this we need to be proactive in developing a positive relationship with their parents. This relationship starts the first time we speak to them. Parents are the child's first educators and have extensive knowledge about their child's character, personality, learning style, likes, dislikes, strengths and difficulties. They are their child's greatest advocate and want the best for them.

Along with any preconceived ideas we may have there are also many anxieties around when we first meet parents. These anxieties influence both sides of the relationship. Parents may have anxieties about whether they are doing the right thing by finding a childcare place at all, never mind finding the right place for their child. As parents we are also very quick to hear any suggestion or implication that we are not 'good' parents. Leaving your child with a professional childcarer can therefore be very daunting. From the practitioners' point of view, each parent who visits the setting is making a judgement about the quality of what we do, and the ways in which we look after their child. This first encounter is surrounded with adult concern and anxiety, something the child, if present, will pick up on but be unlikely to understand. The child may, however, identify the anxiety with the context of being at the setting, which may make the settling-in period more difficult. For the parents of a child with an additional need, however minor or major, the whole process is charged with considerably more anxiety. This may be focused on the likelihood of their child and them being rejected, criticised or even ridiculed. They may even have had such experiences at other settings before visiting yours.

As practitioners we have the opportunity to think about those initial contacts with parents and work to improve them because we go through the process so many times. It is our role to identify good practice and ensure that we do everything we can to make the beginning of our relationship with parents a positive one.

One approach which can start things off in an effective way is to think about the relationship as a journey. This journey is concerned with learning about the child's

- strengths

- pleasures

- concerns

- challenges.

In order to support the child to settle well in the nursery or pre-school, this journey must start with recognition of the extensive knowledge which parents already hold about their children. It is worth while to review our admission and information-gathering procedures on a regular basis and to include parents in the process. Finding quick and easy ways to listen to the views parents have about what works well for them, when they come to visit or are asked to share information, helps to identify good practice which can then be developed and improved.

It would be very surprising if all parents felt that one particular way of involving them would be preferable. We have to find a variety of ways to engage their interest and communicate our willingness to include them in the experiences of their child in our setting. For some parents this may be spending a significant amount of time in the setting once a year to share a talent or skill; for others it could be arriving a few minutes early on one day a week to collect their child so that they can look at photographs and activities which are part of life in the setting. Our goal in each of these opportunities should be to highlight the positive and to make the experience one which everyone would like to repeat. Each small amount of time spent in the setting by a parent provides a chance to encourage and improve the partnership. The most effective way of increasing parents' involvement in their child's life at the setting is to focus on developing a shared knowledge and understanding of the child as a developing personality.

The learning journey, then, encompasses the child's learning and the adults' learning about the child. Each element of contact with parents needs to be reviewed in relation to good practice. For example, where English is an additional language for a family, the challenge for us is to find out from the family the ways in which we can best give and receive information. This does not always mean translating everything we write but may involve taking time to ensure that the message which was intended has been received. From the child's perspective, having keywords recognised or offered, using photographs to support initial understanding and celebrating specific achievements are all possible ways of giving a welcoming message and learning about the child. Generally, in our setting, it is important to consider the images and messages we give about respecting all families from whichever ethnic group or heritage and working to increase our understanding of others. The Race Relations Amendment Act 2000 and the Disability Discrimination Act 1995 both clearly require us to be not just welcoming but actively committed to finding ways to ensure our setting has a culture of valuing and respecting all individuals. With so many children experiencing childcare, we will obviously influence these future adults in the development of their understanding of relationships, in group situations, and the values which can make this a positive experience.

To support new or inexperienced staff it can be very effective to give examples of things to say which fit with the agreed idea of good practice. This process helps all members of staff to review their own scripts and reflect on ways to improve. This can be done in relation to specific situations such as:

- first contact

- admission procedure

- messages we want to give (being explicitly inclusive).

The next stage in the process is to ensure consistency throughout different opportunities which arise for communication:

- daily contact

- parents' evenings

- noticeboards

- newsletters

- phone calls

- letters.

No doubt there will be some relationships between parents and practitioners which will be established more quickly or easily than others. The responsibility for maintaining positive communication links, though, remains with the practitioners as part of their professional role. One of the major challenges to these communication links is when there is a difficult situation which needs to be discussed and resolved. If we can consistently work towards improving our relationship with parents, on a daily basis, we can minimise the difficulty there will be in having the more sensitive and controversial discussions which will inevitably happen. In the same way that we are able to start afresh with each child each day, giving youngsters the opportunity to move on from previous difficulties, as professionals we need to support adults, parents and colleagues in the same way. The other benefit will be that parents will be less anxious in coming to speak to us, share their concerns and be prepared to consider our views because they have belief in our wish to do the best for their child.

One of the most difficult conversations we are likely to need to have with parents is in the situation where we see behaviours and responses which, in our professional view, give us cause for concern about the child's development and this does not coincide with the parents' view. This is where it is essential to consider our relationship with parents as a journey. If the first time we invite the parents to come to talk to us is a formal invitation focusing on our concerns, then we set ourselves up for a very anxious and defensive interaction – in terms of both our feelings and the parents'. However, if we have continually shared observations, planning and strategies relating to the individual child and invited parents' views and their own observations, we are much more likely to have a shared understanding of when and if we need to be concerned. If we can agree that there is cause for concern, we are then more likely to be able to agree on a way forward which will be supported both at home and in the setting. This stage in the journey also paves the way for talking about the involvement of other agencies and professionals. The key message which is the thread throughout this process is that actions are being taken with the child's best interests at the centre of everyone's thinking. The evidence which supports these conversations is inevitably our observations.

These observations need to be effective in identifying what is significant for the particular child. For example, the collation of our observations in their Foundation Stage Record should communicate the essence of the child as an individual. It should evidence understanding of the child's personality, motivation, likes and dislikes. Through indication of levels of involvement in activities we can show strengths, preferred approaches and learning styles. All of this information combines to build a picture of the child's development and progress. Sharing each new discovery about a child provides the opportunity for parents to consider the child's responses to situations at home in a similar light. Enabling and empowering parents to contribute to children's records through their own observations, photographs, etc. gives a richness to the record which makes it something to be valued by child, family and practitioner.

There are several different structures and approaches for focusing and making observations. Kate Wall, in her book *Special Needs and Early Years* (2006), discusses in detail five specific methods. There is discussion of spontaneous observations, recorded in response to a practitioner noticing a child doing something – which could be described as evidence of learning – which is significant for that particular child. This is the form of observation which is most commonly used on a day-to-day basis. These observations are usually dated, recorded on a sticky label and then included directly in the child's Foundation Stage Record. This basic form of observation can be developed to give information about patterns of behaviour and involvement in activities by making the observation at regular time intervals. For example, observing for 1 minute every 15 minutes for 1 hour. Any time interval can be used and the choice will be dictated by the planned purpose for the observation. The likely process leading to a planned observation will be:

- Concern or anomaly noted through standard setting observation process.

- Discussion with other staff, room leader, SENCO, etc.

- Agreement about what further information could be helpful, for example:

  - How often does this occur?

  - Does it happen every day, every morning, etc.?

  - Where does it usually occur?

  - Who else is there when it occurs?

  - What happens leading up to the situation?

  - What happens after the situation has happened?

- If we are clear what information would be helpful next, then we can decide which form of observation would be most useful.

This suggests that observations are only focused on individual children. However, there will also be times when it is useful to look at the way in which children are using the activities which are available in the room. We can do this simply by counting the number of children at each activity at set times or tracking children's movement between activities.

The model identified in the Effective Early Learning Programme, based on the work of Ferre Laevers, provides a very structured and useful means of judging when deep-level learning is taking place. Having identified when it happens, as professionals we can then begin to look for ways to increase the opportunity and consider the common characteristics in activities which will encourage increased levels of learning. The observation schedules can be used to plot the progress of either individuals or groups of children. This provides the possibility of comparing the levels of involvement in different areas of the curriculum, inside, outside and in different areas of the setting. Through this process there is also the means to evaluate the levels of engagement of the adults thereby encouraging reflective thinking about our responses and whether they support or inhibit the children's learning in a specific situation. This is particularly relevant to children with additional needs.

We often suggest that in order to meet the needs of individual children we need more adult time available for them. Through careful observation and reflective thinking we are often able to focus the time which we already have available in more effective ways. A particular concern would also be that more adult attention focused on one child may inhibit their natural relationships with other children and reduce the motivation for the child to try things independently. The adult, if specifically allocated to support an individual child, is also liable to feel responsible for all the child's actions and unconsciously feel they need to justify their role through helping the child more than is strictly necessary. The communication with parents can also be seen as this adult's responsibility or, alternatively, this adult may not be seen as a 'real' member of the team so have no role in communicating with the parent. It is essential that the principle of all children being the responsibility of all practitioners is maintained. The role of the keyworker is then to provide and communicate relevant information to support the shared responsibility.

If we ensure that parents are introduced to the idea of our observation processes at the beginning of our relationship with them, these can then form a secure basis to discuss children's progress. This idea that we do observations needs to be extended to include what information we get from them and how we use the information. Encouraging the parents to share their own observations can be a very effective way of having a shared journey that focuses on getting to know the child and their abilities. As a principle, it is really important that observation notes are phrased positively: state facts and do not record judgements. Using words such as 'very' or 'only' immediately suggests that the child is not meeting your expectations. It is more helpful to record exactly what you see then discuss the implications and assessment later. For example:

*Alesha put 2 out of 5 bricks on the tower following the colour pattern.*

Our assessment can then focus on what further experiences Alesha needs, or what the adults need to do to help Alesha to extend her learning. The assessment may be that:

- Alesha may find this activity easier if the bricks were on the floor rather than the table.

- Larger or smaller bricks may make it easier.

- Items other than bricks would be more motivating for Alesha.

- Being involved with another child in the activity will give Alesha more confidence to play with the bricks and the idea of patterns.

- Laying equipment in a line rather than a tower may make it easier.

From our observation evidence we can have a positive discussion with both colleagues and parents about ways in which we can extend Alesha's current learning. This provides the opportunity for each adult to contribute suggestions from their own experience of Alesha and her learning in other contexts. It is important to remember, also, that often children can display higher skill levels at home than in a setting because they are more relaxed, using their own equipment and with very predictable and familiar adults. Our perspective as adults must always be to look for ways in which we can give children the best possible chance to succeed in the learning they are currently focused on.

This is hardest when the concern is around behaviour, as sometimes we can be drawn into negative feelings about a particular child's behaviour. We then begin to look for the child indulging in the unwanted behaviour to prove that our opinions are right. This is when it makes a difference if our general practice is in making non-judgemental observations and looking for ways to support future learning.

One of the contentious issues which frequently arises when supporting individual children is that of physical safety, either in relation to them hurting themselves through falling, running away, etc. or them hurting others. As with our approach to the safety of all children we would need to consider carefully a risk assessment so that we can identify and minimise the risks involved. However, it is important to maintain a realistic view of the extent to which we can provide a safe environment, and it is essential that all parents are aware of the risk assessment process which is in use. It is not possible or desirable to keep children away from any potential source of harm because, in doing so, we would be unable to:

- encourage a baby to take their first steps

- allow children access to toys

- allow children to feed themselves

- let children play outside

- provide equipment for use in the role-play area

- help children to learn to use stairs

- let children within arm's reach of each other or an adult.

**Understanding how the child is feeling helps us
to sensitively support their learning**

This may sound over-cautious but it is important that parents are included in the discussions and actions taken in trying to ensure an appropriate balance of safety and practical learning about risk taking. As a parent leaving your child at an early years provision, you undoubtedly want to be reassured that your son or daughter will be safe. You are likely to believe that you are the best person to make sure that this happens. However, as your child grows they will need to learn to take increasing responsibility for themselves. There is a huge amount of learning involved in this process. As adults we still get it wrong sometimes, so our learning is continuing.

Seeing dealing with risk as a learning opportunity and part of the journey to independence is probably easier from a practitioner's perspective than a parental one because we do not have the same level of emotional involvement. We also have had more opportunity to develop our comparative view of the ways in which a child is likely to respond to a situation and the relative likelihood of an accident happening in particular situations when considered in the context of the number of children we have worked with during our career. Our role as practitioners is about helping children to have learning experiences which will build towards them being able to become as independent as possible and this includes making inappropriate choices and experiencing the consequences of these on some occasions. One of the initial discussions with parents could be about looking at the provision in the settings and talking about the learning which can be developed through the child's play. This is the time when parents can often give indications of which equipment or experiences would cause them most anxiety. This provides the opportunity for further discussion about the ways in which practitioners consider and manage the risks involved. This is a situation where practitioners need to be sensitive to the variety of reasons why parents may be anxious. For example, they may:

- have had an accident as a child themselves relating to the activity

- have heard of another child who has been hurt or frightened while involved in the activity – perhaps through the media

- have specific concerns about their own child's level of understanding about the dangers/risks in situations

- be particularly protective of their child because of early experiences of the child being vulnerable through illness, premature birth, etc.

No matter how we, as practitioners, feel about the level of risk for the child, we do need take account of the parents' anxiety. We should be proactive in finding ways to involve them in decisions and experiences which will support them to feel that the risk is manageable and the learning valuable for their child. As part of this process there is a clear opportunity for practitioners to review carefully the activity and the way we make it available for children, being clear that our risk assessment is recent and valid for this group of children and adults.

The ideal is for the parents then to be able to spend some time in the setting to see for themselves the children and adults' response to the particular activity. Meeting afterwards, the practitioner is able to talk through the shared experience, identifying key evidence of learning and planning for the next time children use the equipment. Involving parents in learning about safety and risk from the start is really important in ensuring joint parent–practitioner confidence and support for the child. The evidence of the child's progress is then collected through our observations, the identified next steps, details of adult actions, effective strategies and evaluations. Using these as the basis for building on progress is as important for developing independence as any other area of learning.

Undoubtedly, some parents will have more time, energy and enthusiasm for getting involved in the life of the setting than others. As practitioners, we need to maintain the imperative of supporting positive relationships with all parents, through encouraging whatever level of involvement they are able to offer. In our invitations to parents we can communicate clearly that we understand that there are a variety of levels of involvement and that all of these are welcomed and valued. It is our role to promote 'one off' visits around a specific activity, occasional 'drop in' opportunities and regular, sustained joint activities which involve parents. Asking your current group of parents for their views and ideas of opportunities they would be able/happy to take part in to increase their involvement in the setting community is a useful starting point. This may not always be about being with the children in the setting; it may be that parents can support with more adult-orientated activities. Participation could be practical – designing/organising fundraising, sharing decisions about equipment purchase around a specific focus such as developing the outdoor area. Alternatively, it could be about being able to take part as equals in training opportunities which are offered for practitioners. The starting point for this could be having discussions with current or new parents which focus on finding ways to share our knowledge and learning journey with them. As a specific part of this discussion we can identify opportunity for joint practitioner–parent training. Initially this could be a one-off experience around a specific topic such as healthy eating, toilet training, supporting behavioural learning, creative activities, local places which are accessible and child friendly, Bookstart and library activities. All of these can begin with outside speakers being invited to lead the session. This can be developed to include sessions led by the manager to explore activities which will support a particular area of the curriculum, identifying ways these can be used both at home and in the setting. Positive communication following such a session about the impact on children's learning can increase parents' confidence in the role they can play in the learning which takes place in the setting.

For parents who are unable to attend the sessions it would be important to include them through other means such as a newsletter, photographs, displays with annotation or PowerPoint slide shows. These forms of communication can be provided jointly by a practitioner and a parent who did attend the session. From our knowledge of the current group of parents involved in our setting, we can identify any preferences for translation or interpretation. This should not just be an afterthought but part of the planning discussion with the parents concerned. If we are proactive in asking parents what would help to make such a training session accessible for them and explaining that we will find a way to provide what is needed, they are more likely to feel welcomed and valued and this will increase the likelihood of them attending.

## Key points

- Involving parents in the life of the setting is important and helps the children's learning.

- Several methods of observation can be used to gather specific information which will inform the planning for future learning.

- Risk assessment processes should involve parents, and practitioners can be proactive in developing a joint understanding of the activity/situation and steps which are taken to ensure reasonable safety levels.

- Parents' levels of involvement with settings will vary considerably depending on many factors. The practitioners' role is to encourage and communicate the variety of possible ways in which the parents could be involved. This will range from one-off visits to joint parent–practitioner training.

## Parents' views

There are several ways to gather parents' views about things without always using a questionnaire. For example:

- Post-it note display, e.g. ideas for outings, things I like to do with my child.

- Sticky name cards to place on display, e.g. I would like you to contact me by phone, face to face, email, etc.

- Pebbles in a container, e.g. choice of next parents' evening being about healthy eating or bedtimes.

- Laptop/Computer photograph display, e.g. things my child likes doing at nursery/home.

- Suggested foods for the menu with 'tick' voting system.

## More in-depth parents' views

When you first met the team at our nursery:

- what did we do which made you feel welcome?

- what else could we have done to make you feel more welcome?

- did we give you enough/too much/ too little information about what we do?

Now that you know us better:

- do we give you about the right amount of information you want on your child?

- is there any other information you would like us to give you?

- what is the best way for us to give you news about things which are going on in the nursery?

- would it be helpful for us to get information translated into another language for you?

- would it be helpful for us to get someone to interpret for you when we meet?

- what would you like to see us do next to improve our relationship with you?

- what would you like to see us work harder at as a staff team?

# CHAPTER 4

# Language development

Language development is a key component of children's early learning. We are beginning to learn more about the very early communication involving babies from before they are born and in the first few minutes of life. Practitioners have a significant role to play in providing opportunities and interactions which encourage language and communication development.

Playing

**Sharing**

**Taking**

**Giving back**

**Giving another container**

The early language experiences of children have changed dramatically over recent years. However, I doubt if there was ever a 'golden age' when all children had access to rich language experiences. Common sense tells us that if children are exposed to, and involved in, positive language experiences with sensitive adults, they will have the best possible chance of developing their own language. If we were to consider all of the skills, knowledge and technicalities which children have to learn before they are able to be skilful communicators, we would not believe it possible that anyone could learn to use language! Just a simple list makes it seem daunting. A child needs to be able to:

- remember

- recall

- learn

- organise and hold in mind a series of ideas

- control muscles of the mouth

- control breathing

- imitate

- hear and discriminate between sounds

- produce sounds

- link sounds with meaning.

Our experience would suggest that children are generally highly motivated to use language to communicate. Given encouragement and appropriate modelling most children develop their language skills effectively. One of the key pieces of evidence for this is that the development of language in infancy is directly influenced by 'local' language or regional accents. This exposure to language is not just about hearing the words; it is a much more complex process. The exploration of this complexity can begin to help us make conscious decisions about the language experiences our children have day to day. For example, the importance of language modelling being a reciprocal interaction at an appropriate level of difficulty challenges what children are likely to learn from extended television watching or mainly instruction-giving language in a childcare setting.

Communication is integral to establishing and maintaining relationships. This communication is strongly supported through language, although it is important to note that this is not necessarily verbal language and can be British Sign Language. The key is that it is a means through which we can convey information, including:

- wants

- desires

- emotions

- facts

in a two-way flow between the producer and the receiver or receivers. As adults working with children we are in a prime position to provide quality learning opportunities supported by positive adult interactions which will effectively facilitate children's language development. In order to do this well we need to understand the process and extend our own knowledge of the language acquisition process. This chapter highlights some of the key factors but further reading is necessary to supplement it. A specific source of information which will develop your understanding is the *Birth to Three Matters* (Sure Start, 2002) materials. Although most practitioners are now very familiar with the cards in the *Birth to Three* pack, few seem to have had the opportunity to explore in detail the CD included in the pack. It is a rich source of information, suggestions and examples from childcare settings.

## Background

Babies are born with the survival instinct to communicate their needs and to have these needs met. Newborns learn about rhythmic properties of main carers' language, sounds and movement. These become familiar and predictable over time so providing communication of what is likely to happen next. Some sounds or movements become linked with providing comfort, warning or encouragement. A focus of research over recent years has been to explore the communication which may take place while the baby is still in the womb (Karmiloff and Karmiloff-Smith, 2001; Sure Start, 2002). Undoubtedly, there is still a lot for us to learn about language and its development, particularly in relation to those very early experiences. Babies begin to make sounds from the time they are born and receive a response to those sounds. As a rough guide to babies' developing relationship with sound:

- 0–3 months – produce non-speech sounds

- 3–4 months – produce vowel-like sounds

- 0–4 months – able to discriminate sound contrasts of all languages

- 9 months – recognise specific sound combinations.

Such guides do not mean that each stage will or should be achieved within the age range but that our research and experience would suggest that the majority of children will acquire this learning within this time frame. However, in the case of language, current thinking would indicate that there are identifiable 'windows of opportunity' for the development of particular skills. This is not to say that this is the only time that these skills will develop, but it provides an optimum time for children to take advantage of specific learning opportunities. As the majority of language and conceptual learning takes place in infancy, this means that there is a significant responsibility for those working in childcare provision.

Research by Colwyn Trevarthen (1993) explores the evidence that within minutes of being born children are involved in two-way communication with adults using both noises and body language. One of the key elements of this two-way communication is that it must be reciprocal. The baby reacts very differently to a response that reacts to their own communication than to one which does not. Trevarthen explored this by videoing a mother involved in a reciprocal interaction, making sounds and facial expressions which were in tune with her child's responses. He then replayed the video to the baby without the mother present. The child could see the same reactions but they were no longer reactive to how the child was feeling. The child in this situation lost interest within seconds. Trevarthen suggests that this is evidence that the responses of the adult need to be 'tuned in' to the baby's current communications. From this reciprocal experience children begin developing ways of communicating their needs and wants.

Babies who are deprived of this reciprocal relationship, where the adult is proactive in tuning in and initiating communication, are likely to give up trying to get a response from the adult if it continues over an extended period of time.

It is important for all children that we realise that speech development is only one element of the broader learning about communication. The links between thought and language are very complex. In the development of both, access to a rich learning environment and a sensitive learning companion is essential. As adults, our role is firstly as interpreter, learning about individual children and the way they indicate if they are hungry, distressed or happy. The sharing of this knowledge and understanding, with adults at home, enables us to give children more consistent responses and encourage their attempts at communication. Building a record of the child's current communication, possibly through photographs, is one way of ensuring that parents feel involved in their child's life at the setting. Examples can be included from both home and the setting to really make it relevant to the child's development and give every opportunity for the adults to work together in encouraging the child's next steps in language development. Using these examples and our usual observations also provides vital information about the rate of progress for the child. Dating every piece of evidence relating to the child's development is essential (including the year) along with an indication of the context in which the observed activity took place. Often this rate of progress can be one of the first indicators that the child is either acquiring skills more or less quickly than would be expected.

Learning in any area of the curriculum is most likely to occur where a child is feeling relaxed, joyful and experiencing high levels of involvement in an activity. Our observations and interactions with the child become richer if we note the signals which the child gives us to indicate when they are really involved and enjoying an activity. Ferre Laevers, in his research which underpins the Effective Early Learning Programme, identifies the following signals which indicate that a child is involved in an activity:

- Concentration – attention solely directed at activity.

- Energy – child is investing a lot of energy and is eager and stimulated.

- Complexity and creativity – working at the edge of their capabilities and exhibits individuality in the activity.

- Facial expression and posture – duration of concentration at activity, wanting to continue and put in effort.

- Precision – attention to detail.

- Reaction time – alert and reacts quickly to stimuli.

- Language – language used shows importance of activity.

- Satisfaction – pleased with what they have done.

As we get to know individual children we are increasingly aware of how they would communicate and show these signals of involvement. The expectation is not that the children will continually show these signals but that we begin to identify the situations in which they are most likely to be able to get this involved in their learning.

Through our developing knowledge of an individual child we are able to take advantage of situations where we know the child will be most relaxed and motivated. We can then focus on identifying ways to sensitively support new learning. For very young babies, it is important to consider the opportunities we offer for them to physically move around to access an activity or piece of equipment, or gain proximity to other children or adults. These are key ways in which babies communicate their interest and choice. The use of treasure baskets for young babies is an ideal opportunity to look for signals which indicate interest in a particular object. Having identified this interest we are then able to plan our own responses and other opportunities we can provide to enable the child's learning to progress through this interest. We can also begin to add our own language to the child's responses. This personalises some of the child's first experiences of language and can provide a motivator for early attempts at speech. One of the most influential effects on a child's language is adult modelling and support in early understanding and positive responses to attempts at vocalisation. This is true whether a child has any specific difficulties or not. Using routine activities such as getting dressed, eating, drinking, etc. as times to talk about objects, likes and dislikes, models appropriate language and reinforces appropriate vocabulary. Our key aim is to give a positive response to a child's vocalisation and to encourage more. Using these routine times can also highlight the link between word, context and meaning for the child. All the children we work with will develop at a different pace, respond differently to particular situations and gain skills and knowledge in different ways and at different rates. We are all individuals with different experiences and styles of learning.

As well as encouraging and modelling the speech element of communication children need to experience being listened to and listening to sounds. Being able to give a baby periods of undivided attention as part of the process of tuning in will provide a deeper quality to the relationship.

> *The implications of the research findings which lead to the above statements about babies and young children as skilful communicators and the importance of being together are primarily that they need relaxed, playful and loving conversations right from birth.* (Sure Start, 2002, Literature review, p. 69)

The use of rhymes and rhythms as part of the sharing of language play are particularly important in letting the child explore and experience how language fits together. It allows internalisation of the form of language without the immediate need for understanding each individual word. There are also more subtle benefits to the sharing of rhyme and rhythm activities in that it provides a way of strengthening the relationship between those involved. The shared experience, eye contact, body language and reciprocal signals can clearly communicate the enjoyment participants are experiencing. This is also an activity which can encourage closer partnership with parents. Finding out about rhymes which are, or have been, used within the family, having them on tape and learning them for use in the setting can be a very proactive way to link home and setting experiences for the child. It is also useful in showing value and respect for family culture.

Once the child begins to offer language and specific words, the adults can continue the positive encouragement and increase the modelling of appropriate language. As they explore new language children will inevitably make mistakes and our response in this situation is very important. We need to be giving consistent messages in encouraging attempts at producing language through our expression, body language and verbal response. We can also provide the corrected language in reflecting back our understanding of what the child has said. This needs to be done sensitively without implying that the child has done something wrong which could stop them trying next time.

For example, if the child says 'I goed to the park', a response might be: 'You went to the park? What did you do there?' This provides the corrected response, extends the interaction, shows your interest, shows you have been listening and consolidates the relationship between you both. The same is true of situations where children provide single-word responses. For example, if a child offers one word, 'car', our response could encourage and add to it by saying 'yes, a big car!' Again it is worth reflecting on how important it is to respond showing enthusiasm and pleasure through our facial expression and body language. We all receive more information from non-verbal communication rather than the actual words which are spoken. Children rely heavily on the non-verbal clues, particularly in the early stages of language acquisition, so it is important that we work hard at emphasising our messages about showing interest and enthusiasm for what they are saying.

Levels of understanding and language are often mismatched in the early stages with children being able to pick out one or two keywords and 'reading' the non-verbal communication. Generally speaking, as adults we offer too much language to children when we are giving an instruction so it is useful to consider our usual phrases and to check if they give a clear message and allow the child time to think and carry out the instruction. Photographs of sequences of events can be very helpful to support understanding of instructions and expectations.

Although there are many outlines of the developmental stages of language acquisition, one of the key issues to hold on to is the individual child's progress and that our expectations are realistic for this particular child. There could well be two three-year-olds with vastly different language abilities and our role would be to adjust our language for each child to support their understanding. Our observations of their responses and language they offer provides the detail of their increased understanding and progress.

One element of role modelling which is often overlooked in the busy life of childcare is the way in which the adults speak to each other. Children will learn more from this than any specific teaching we may try to use. If we want children to speak kindly, respectfully and listen to each other, we have to do the same. This is not about remembering one day a week to make a special effort but finding ways to improve our own communication with our colleagues, using the same techniques we use to learn about children. This could include:

- finding out about their interests
- listening to them
- making time to share ideas
- talking about shared experiences
- offering genuine compliments.

By considering how we would like others to communicate with us, we can begin to identify actions which will build more positive relationships with our colleagues.

This role modelling through adult–adult interaction is part of developing a professional persona. Practitioners do not all need to be best friends but do need to be able to work together for the benefit of the children.

One language issue which causes considerable concern for both parents and practitioners is children swearing. I would suggest that the first step is to acknowledge with all parents that at some time their children will hear and try out a variety of words which we feel are not appropriate. In the life of a childcare setting there will periodically be times when the majority of children seem to be using swear words. Often our first response is to try to find the source and to have someone to blame for introducing the particular word or words. However, I would see this as a waste of time and energy. Thinking back to our exploration of language acquisition our response was crucial in encouraging children to use language. The same is true about swearing. If we give a significant attention-filled response, positive or negative, we will inadvertently entrench the use of the swear words. It is far more effective to involve all parents and practitioners in responding in an agreed way if they hear children swearing. Our communication with parents about swearing will be most effective if it is set in the context of children's learning, for example celebrating how well children's language is developing and the ways in which the setting activities support this, and suggesting ways in which language can be encouraged at home. The swearing can then be introduced as a phase which will happen but may be very short-lived for some children, longer for others. A final option might be to share the strategies and approaches which are being employed in the setting and offer the opportunity to discuss individual concerns with parents.

This agreed response should be shared in as much detail as possible, including possible phrases which could be used by the adult. Initially children use swear words without knowing they are inappropriate so by playing down our response and distracting by praising appropriate words we can minimise the motivation to repeat the swearing.

A later stage is characterised by children realising that the words are not acceptable but very effective in getting a reaction from adults. Often practitioners find themselves saying that the child knows what they are saying and that it is not acceptable. This is not quite the case I don't think. My view would be that the adult's response has given the child the message that using swear words is a guaranteed way of getting undivided attention and, even if this is negative, it is better than no attention.

There also needs to be a general increase in the praise level for appropriate language through commenting on acceptable words and phrases for all children. With pre-school age children this may also include making a collection of words and phrases which we use to communicate our anger, frustration, excitement, etc.

Photographs are essential in sharing information, providing clarity for instructions, helping children to understand what is going to happen next and as a record of the current level of learning. Increasingly, practitioners are also using sign systems such as Makaton or Sign and Say which support children's understanding of the spoken language and encourage verbal communication. This use of signs can be very effective in reducing the frustration levels which many children experience when they are unable to make their needs, wants and emotions clear.

If, from our observations, we feel that a child's language is not developing as we and their parents would expect, it is useful to eliminate some basic possibilities. For example:

- Is the child able to hear not just sounds but different pitch and tone?

- Do they have frequent colds which could be affecting the quality of their hearing?

- Are they offering more verbal language in other situations?

- Are they physically able to produce sounds?

As the evidence of concern and discussion with parents increases, the next step is to discuss with a health professional such as the Health Visitor, Doctor or Speech and Language Therapist. These professionals will be able to focus on any specific reasons why the child may be having difficulty. Their suggested strategies will then supplement the specific language development opportunities you are continuing to provide for the child. The information from other professionals will guide your differentiation of both the activity and the language offered/expected by adults. For example, you might choose rhymes and rhythms, which emphasize particular sounds or combination of sounds, to help the child begin to notice the contrast or similarity of them.

Our expectations of children's development and response to this rich language environment is informed by our knowledge of child development and our knowledge of individual children, their particular rates of progress and abilities. The Early Years Foundation Stage document (DfES, 2006), as also in Birth to Three Frameworks, details some of the expected milestones and developmental expectations. These have been summarised in Table 4.1.

We often hear of the importance of providing a rich language environment for our children and sometimes it is hard to identify specific elements which would fit with this description. I would not advocate a checklist approach because the most important factor is the way in which the elements are used and shared with children. However, the Early Years Foundation Stage document does suggest the following:

- *Providing opportunities for children to communicate thoughts, ideas and feelings and build up relationships with adults and each other*

- *Giving opportunities to share and enjoy a wide range of rhymes, music, songs, poetry, stories and non-fiction books*

- *Giving opportunities for linking language with physical movement in action songs and rhymes, role play and practical experiences such as cookery and gardening*

- *Planning an environment that reflects the importance of language through signs, notices and books*

- *Providing opportunities for children to see adults writing and for children to experiment with writing for themselves through making marks, personal writing symbols and conventional script*

- *Providing time and opportunities to develop spoken language through conversation between children and adults, both one to one and in small groups, with particular awareness of, and sensitivity to, the needs of children learning English as an additional language, using their home language when appropriate*

- *Providing time and opportunities for children to develop their phonological awareness through small group and individual teaching, when appropriate*

Table 4.1 Expected milestones and developmental expectations in the early years

| Age range | Typical development characteristics |
| --- | --- |
| Birth to 11 months | Beginning to communicate in a variety of ways, crying, smiling, babbling, squealing to indicate needs |
| 8–20 months | Using vocalisation, movement and expressions to make needs and feelings known |
| 16–26 months | Beginning of single-word and sign/symbol use for intentional communication of needs and feelings |
| 22–26 months | Significant increase in number of words and sign/symbols used to communicate about things which interest them |
| 30–50 months | Linking words and statements, intonation and tone developing. Engaging in familiar rhymes/rhythms |
| | Following instructions, understanding and involvement in stories, beginning questioning. Listening to others, turn taking in conversations. Significant increase in vocabulary, particularly around topics and people important to them |
| | Beginning to indicate possession through language. Use of language reflects breadth of experience and involvement in activities |
| 40–60+ months | Increased confidence in speaking to others, uses talk to gain attention, starts conversation, listens to others, maintains theme in own communication. Uses language, signs and symbols for increasing range of purposes |

Source: Adapted from Early Years Foundation Stage consultation document (DfES, 2006)

■ *Planning opportunities for all children to become aware of languages and writing systems other than English, and communication systems such as signing and Braille*

■ *Early identification of and response to any particular difficulties in children's language development*

■ *Close teamwork between bilingual workers, speech therapists and practitioners, where appropriate*

■ *Opportunities for children who use alternative communication systems to develop ways of recording and accessing texts to develop their skills in these methods*

(DfES, 2006, p. 42)

Taking account of the developmental milestones and the good practice suggestions provides the range of possible activities which can be employed to support a child whose language is not developing as quickly or in the way we would have expected. The same observation, assessment and next steps approach applies, ensuring that parents are involved and that the next steps are small enough.

 ## Key points

■ Babies begin communicating even before they are born.

■ Providing an interactive and rich language environment will support children's learning.

■ Children may not communicate verbally but may use sign language such as British Sign Language. The same principles would apply in encouraging communication with adults, children and in display around the setting.

■ Makaton or Sign and Say signing, which encourages language development, can reduce frustration levels as children acquire vocabulary.

■ The interaction with positive, sensitive adults using appropriate vocabulary is crucial in extending children's language experience.

■ Although expected milestones can be identified, knowledge of the individual child provides the basis for planning next steps and individual learning.

■ Sharing observations and next steps with parents provides a context for finding ways of giving individual children the best possible chance of increasing their confidence in use of language.

## Things to think about

What exactly are your concerns about the child's language?

Do they relate to:

- the actual sounds the child makes?

- the word order the child uses?

- the time it takes for the child to think of particular words to use?

- the naming of things and categories of things?

- the child's understanding of what someone says to them?

## What could be affecting the child's language development?

- Is the child able to hear sounds of different pitch and tone?

- Do they have frequent colds which could be affecting the quality of their hearing?

- Do they offer more language in some situations than others?

- Are they physically able to produce a range of sounds?

- What range of experience of being talked to, sung to, read to and encouragement to talk has the child had?

- Does the child show any signs of anxiety or shyness?

- Are there any emotional reasons why the child would not want to speak in front of others?

# CHAPTER 5

# Behaviour

We need to make conscious decisions about what we think about behaviour and how we are going to help children learn about it. There are some milestones in children's developmental understanding of behaviour which we should take into account when setting our expectations. Thinking of behavioural learning in the same way as other areas of learning and involving parents in the process of agreeing next steps gives a useful framework for discussions. Conflict resolution is a hard skill to learn but being consistent in our approach increases the likelihood of children using the process. Next steps can be more effectively set if they are based on 'can do' statements formulated from observations.

We all come into the childcare profession with a range of experiences, attitudes and knowledge. Behaviour is probably the most contentious and controversial area to be discussed between childcare practitioners. Often our views are a direct consequence of our own childhood experiences. While we can move our thinking on in relation to other areas of the curriculum, our views on behaviour are so wrapped up in our beliefs and value systems we find it really difficult to find our 'professional view' in the maze of our personal views. This becomes increasingly evident the more anxious or challenged we feel. As things get more difficult we retreat further into the familiar personal views which we hold.

My suggestion would be that the most effective way of thinking consistently about behaviour is to use the model of thinking which we use for every other area of the curriculum. Firstly, behaviour means everything we say and everything we do, not just inappropriate behaviour. It is an area of learning like any other for which the following observations are true:

- The pace of our learning varies.

- We will learn through imitation, play, role play, trial and error, involvement in experiential learning opportunities, response and reward, and direct teaching.

- Our experiences vary considerably.

- Our learning can be planned for.

- Appropriate and manageable next steps for learning can be identified.

- Appropriate support from sensitive adults will increase the pace of our learning.

- There will be observable evidence of our learning.

- Our understanding and ability is influenced by our development and maturation.

- Consistent responses and messages will increase the pace of our learning.

Our behaviour is integral to our communication particularly before we have mastered fluency in language. As very young babies we show our reaction to certain situations through our behaviour and receive a particular response. We cry and are fed, for example. This process relies on an adult being tuned in to our behaviour and, rather than getting cross that we are crying, is able to interpret that we are hungry. This sounds so simple when thinking about a young baby but is more complex as we get older. Our communication becomes more complex, the possibilities of what we are trying to communicate become greater and the number of adults we are involved with also increases. Table 5.1 gives a rough outline of some of the developmental milestones which we experience as children.

These indications of some of the developmental milestones which occur begin to help us consider how realistic some of our expectations are in our day-to-day dealing with children. For example, it would be surprising if a child of two years old was able to understand the conditions under which particular emotions would be experienced. But we often assume that toddlers are making conscious decisions about their behaviour when the reality is that they are reacting to our behaviour which we are not consciously thinking about! This could well be the explanation for much of children's behaviour which we dismiss as 'attention seeking'. If we only give attention to children when they behave inappropriately, then we are teaching them to behave inappropriately to get our attention.

The amount of learning which takes place for children in their very early years in relation to behaviour is incredible and it is amazing the extent to which children do understand their own and other people's behaviour. The milestones in Table 5.1 are strongly influenced by the presence of a sensitive carer who is able to offer reciprocal responses to the baby's communication and behaviour. This intimate relationship is integral to the baby's developing understanding about relationships, behaviour and communication. Initially, it is likely that this relationship will be between the mother and the baby. In terms of an early years setting this is likely to be the keyworker. The importance of this relationship cannot be over-emphasised. The support needed for practitioners, particularly those who are young or inexperienced, to enable them to be able to sustain such relationships in partnership with the parents, needs to be carefully thought through, planned for and discussed with parents.

It is often helpful to explore and identify some key messages which, as a setting, you would like to communicate specifically about behaviour. For example:

- Appropriate behaviour will be noticed and commented on more than inappropriate behaviour.

- Learning opportunities will be based on what the children can do.

- Any 'rules' will be phrased positively to highlight what children need to do rather than what they should not do.

- Adults will role model appropriate behaviour in their daily activities with each other, including a variety of ways to share and take turns.

- Parents will be involved in reviewing observations and next steps for children's behavioural learning.

## Table 5.1 Some developmental milestones in behavioural learning from birth to 10 years

| Age | Developmental milestones |
|---|---|
| Newborns | Distinguish mother's voice from another. From 1 hour to 6 weeks of life – imitate simple movement of the face, head and hand modelled by an adult |
| 2–3 days | Discriminate between mother's face and stranger's |
| 6 weeks | Reproduce facial movement presented by novel social partner after 24 hours |
| 7 weeks | Visual scanning tends to concentrate in eye region |
| 10 weeks | Social behaviour changes appropriately and non-imitatively in response to different facial expressions of their carer. Intersubjective activities such as joint attention, joint emotion |
| 2 months | Turn taking, face-to-face interaction |
| 2.5–3 months | Social smiles produced in response to another person's smile |
| 4–5 months | Discriminate between emotional expressions (facial and vocal in combination before vocal or facial alone) |
| 7 months | Recognise emotional expressions (happy and angry) |
| 8 months | Will respond to request to show an adult a toy |
| 9 months | Able to co-ordinate interacting with objects and people at the same time |
| 9–10 months | Social referencing |
| 18 months | Start to pretend. Relationships/friendships outside the family begin to develop |
| 1 year | Attach emotional meaning to a particular object in the environment |
| 2 years | Able to think about things which are absent or hypothetical. Start to understand that intentional states such as feelings or perceptions are directed towards particular targets in the world Able to conjure up imaginary states not confused with reality; desires and beliefs projected on to dolls/soldiers/toys; explain and predict people's behaviour Actively comfort and hurt others, no longer simply reacting; can anticipate bringing about different emotions in other people Engaging in teasing and deception Most two-year-olds realise you can tell something about how people feel from how they look or behave |
| 2.5 years | Start to understand that desires drive our behaviour |
| 2–3 years | Emotional state becomes a goal in itself; actively try to change another person's emotional state – don't necessarily experience similar emotion Understand the connection between desires and actions |
| 3 years | Grasp that their deceptive actions will bring about false belief in another Will predict character actions even when beliefs contrast with their own |
| 3–4 years | Understanding of mental life goes through a conceptual revolution |
| 4–10 years | Begin to understand the conditions under which pride, shame and guilt are experienced |

Source: This information has been collated from Hala (1997), Astington (1993) and Dunn (2004)

- Expectations of children's behaviour will be realistic in the context of their age, stage, ability and understanding.

- Children's behavioural learning will be planned for in the same way as other areas of the curriculum.

- Conflict situations will be used to support behavioural learning.

The next step, having identified a collection of key messages, is to discuss with colleagues what we would see which would tell us that these messages were becoming a reality in our setting. This then gives us a context in which we can increase the likelihood of the children experiencing a consistent and supportive context for their behavioural learning.

In order that as adults we effectively support children's behavioural learning we need to make some conscious decisions about what it is that needs to be learned. Our thoughts around this, as with all other areas of learning, will be informed by the relevant guidance such as the Early Years Foundation Stage document. This clearly guides us with principles and practical ways of supporting the children's learning and the adult action.

To develop a rich learning environment which encourages behavioural learning we need to consider our setting from the perspective of the individual child. This can help us to be explicit about the ways in which we help children to:

- make choices

- communicate their needs appropriately

- access sensitive adults when they need them

- understand about their own feelings

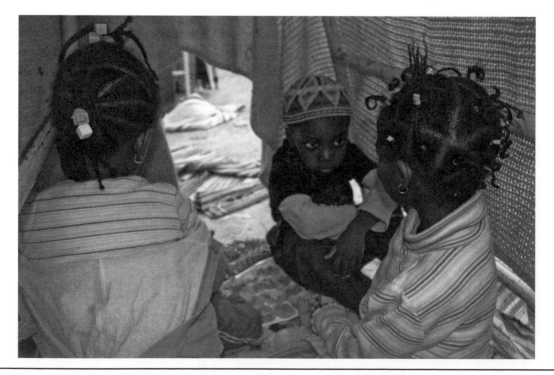

**Role-play opportunities**

■ understand about others' feelings

■ feel confident in the company of others

■ have opportunities for autonomy in their learning.

Considering our routines in the setting in relation to these factors can make a significant difference to the children's experience of the day. The Early Years Foundation Stage document states that:

*Schedules and routines must be responsive to the children's needs, to allow all children to have time to become engrossed and think deeply about what they are doing. Although children need a predictable environment, this does not equate to rigid routines.* (DfES, 2006, p. 8)

Sometimes our routines have a tendency to be driven more by staffing needs for breaks and to maintain ratios rather than for the benefit of the children. Our first consideration should be to identify good practice in the experiences provided for the children. The staffing concerns then need to be addressed to facilitate the improved experiences for the children. One obvious example which relates to behaviour is access to outdoor learning spaces. For many children the very fact that they are able to be involved in a particular activity outside rather than inside will increase their involvement and reduce the likelihood of distraction into inappropriate behaviour. The ideal is that children are able to use both the indoor and the outdoor spaces freely during the majority of the day. Issues of appropriate clothing for either practitioners or children should not prevent this from becoming a reality. Physical difficulties with buildings should be overcome through proactive action planning. It is likely that having free access to outdoor space will increasingly become essential criteria for parents in their choice of setting.

Considering particular areas in the setting can also help to identify opportunities for children to access quiet, calming spaces and activities which we have identified as reassuring for them. Activities which encourage and facilitate children's opportunity to identify and represent their emotions can be very effective for some youngsters. Specific equipment and activities which can enable children to explore, play with and learn about feelings, emotions and behaviour include:

■ puppets

■ pictures of facial expressions for discussion

■ posting boxes to make choices about how they are feeling now

■ stories with particular scenarios which can be talked about

■ photographs from life in the setting which can be discussed in terms of how different people may be feeling

■ games involving talking about how individuals might feel in certain situations

■ role-play and pretend play opportunities.

It is important to recognise that there are no right or wrong answers in identifying facial expressions. Even as adults we cannot be sure if our interpretation of another's expression is accurate unless we can ask the person at the time. Equally, while a particular situation may make me feel frightened, you may find it exciting so all suggestions should be accepted and talked about with encouragement to say more about their thinking than just naming the possible emotion.

Having focused on the physical environment and the ways in which it can support children's behavioural learning, the most crucial influence on children's behavioural learning will be the quality of the interactions with the adults. Over time this builds into the ethos and predictability of the responses the child will expect in certain situations. If generally children are not experiencing positive, responsive, secure, safe relationships with the adults in the setting, their behaviour will change accordingly. They will be likely to respond by trying to gain more individual attention, over-enthusiastically welcoming visitors, seeking support from each other, and their ability to become involved in learning opportunities will be reduced. It can be helpful to review the ways in which we specifically support children's behavioural learning and the current characteristic behavioural responses of children in order to ensure that our planning is based on what children can do and the appropriate next steps both for individuals and for the group as a whole.

From an adult perspective the most challenging behavioural situation to deal with is probably when a conflict occurs between children. Our response is often to take control and impose our own decisions on the situation. This has the effect of stopping the conflict but does not provide the children with any learning about how to deal with the next situation when it arises. First, we have to accept that conflict is an inevitable part of our daily experiences; we will never experience a day with no conflict between children or adults in an early years setting – this is not a realistic expectation. Therefore, we need to make some conscious decisions about how we are going to approach enabling children to learn about effective ways of dealing with conflicts. For practitioners it is helpful to have a system or framework which is agreed and will be used consistently in the setting. For children this will increase the speed of learning and feelings of safety. This adult discussion should include consideration of the following questions:

**Independent snacktime**

- Is it appropriate for children to say sorry after an incident?

- Can more attention be given for appropriate behaviour than inappropriate behaviour in the 'sorting out' process?

- In what ways can we ensure that children receive consistent messages about their behaviour?

- Should children always have to share/take turns with all the equipment/toys they are using?

- Do all children need to be friends all of the time?

- What do we think is acceptable/not acceptable behaviour for particular age ranges in resolving conflict, expressing anger/frustration, taking turns, following adult wishes?

- What influences our decisions about the above with different children?

From this discussion we can bring together a consensus of how we are going to support children's behavioural learning in our setting. We can then apply this to the process of conflict resolution. We want children to have the opportunity over time to learn how to resolve their own conflicts, but it is not realistic to expect this to happen on a regular basis before they reach an age and stage when they can understand the whole process – possibly once they are adults and even then there will be some situations in which they (we!) revert to earlier 'childish' responses. Currently they are learning through trial and error about what will get them their own way and how it feels to be involved in conflict. As with all learning, being told once does not change the behaviour or secure the learning for all situations.

Our agreed resolution process could be based on a variety of approaches, but generally they have the same core outline. For example:

1　Find out what has happened

   – Take turns

   – Listen to each other

2　Reflect what you think has happened

   – Is that right?

3　How can we sort it out?

   – Each person involved has an opportunity to suggest a solution

4　What could we do differently next time?

5　What will we do now?

Following this process provides opportunity for children to experience and see how they can have their say and have a solution which makes everyone moderately happy. The key message is that talking through the situation is a good thing and more effective than hitting, kicking, screaming, etc. It is important that a variety of solutions are available even if some are provided by the adult. This ensures that children are involved in making a choice about which solution would be most effective for them in this situation. Any suggestions for solutions need to be valued and considered, with the children being encouraged to try out the one they think will work. If necessary, the adult can check back later to reflect with the children on whether or not the solution worked. The greater variety of solutions the children experience and try out, the more likely they are to be able to find an appropriate solution in different situations. With older groups it can be useful to collect solutions which have been tried, which can then be referred to; displaying photographs with some annotation can be particularly helpful.

As with every other area of learning, though, some children (and adults!) really struggle with behaviour. Sometimes there are medical conditions or experiences which impact on children's behaviour and make behavioural learning much more difficult. In the same way as we discussed sharing the learning journey with parents in Chapter 3, it is essential to establish a positive relationship with parents and to share our understanding of their child on a regular basis. Behaviour is often a subject people feel they do not wish to discuss in any depth; we feel defensive as if the child's behaviour is our fault and that we should be able to fix it, even when we feel completely overwhelmed and at our wits' end. This is true for parents and practitioners alike at some stage. From our very first conversation with parents we need to show and involve them in our approach to focusing on behavioural learning. We can find out about current ways in which the child uses their behaviour to communicate and compare their responses to different situations.

As a parent generally we want our child to be 'good' but we have not always thought this through in detail or applied it to situations where we are not present. Our children are suddenly exposed to larger numbers of children and adults than they have had to deal with before and we expect them to respond in the same way as they have done with fewer children and adults. Our role as practitioners is to maintain realistic expectations of individual children and to keep focused on helping them to make progress in their behavioural learning. To do this we can share our observations and next steps as we would do for any other area of learning, involving the parents in agreeing the strategies we will use.

One of the major difficulties for behavioural learning is ensuring that we make the next steps small enough and focused enough to give the child the best possible chance of success. A technique which can be helpful is to make a list of 'can do' statements from your observations which can then form the basis of your next steps. If the 'can do' statements contain the following elements:

- observable behaviour

- context

- time

then you will have a statement like this:

*Ahmed can sit still and quiet on the carpet for a story with an adult for one minute.*

This statement can then become a next step by changing just one element, for example:

*Ahmed will sit still and quiet on the carpet for a story with an adult for three minutes.*

Any change to the time needs to be realistic in relation to your knowledge of the individual child, not related to what other children at the setting can currently manage. The next stage is to agree what adult actions need to take place to support Ahmed to achieve the next step. This is likely to include the four 'Ps':

■ Prepare

■ Prompt

■ Practise

■ Praise.

Adults can then agree the ways in which they will help Ahmed to:

■ prepare for storytime, perhaps sharing a photograph of previous enjoyment of storytime

■ prompt, either using gestures (Makaton sign for sit, thumbs up, etc.) or quiet verbal prompts to encourage appropriate responses

■ practise at other times – for example, if Ahmed happens to sit for three minutes during music time or in a smaller group, reflect on how he was able to manage this and link with being able to do this for storytime

■ receive praise – not all children respond well to loud public praise. What is most appropriate and effective for Ahmed?

When agreeing next steps with parents it is useful to consider a realistic timescale within which to review progress and how you will both be able to compare evidence and views of his progress.

If a pattern develops in relation to a particular child's behavioural learning which suggests that there are difficulties in this area, we will have evidence of the 'can do' statements, next steps and adult actions we have used so far. This information is very helpful for communicating exactly what is happening for the child and showing the reasons for concern. If parents have been involved in this process from the beginning, it is more likely that their views and yours will be similar about the level of concern. The discussion then becomes about what further advice or help is available for you both to access. To support the parent with this decision it is helpful if you can accurately explain what the process would involve. For example, would someone come to the setting or home, would the parent have to take the child somewhere, what sort of action might be taken, what information would be recorded and where would it be kept? If you are unsure about the answers to these questions, it can be helpful to check them out before talking to the parent but without giving names or details related to your enquiry until you have the parents' consent.

Once advice from other professionals has been given, it is important that you implement it and maintain the process of observation and review with parents to provide feedback about the effectiveness of the advice or strategies suggested.

Although behaviour is one of the issues which raises the most anxiety it is also the area which is one of the most rewarding to be able to help children learn about.

### Key points

■ Treating behaviour in the same way as other areas of learning helps to provide a planning process for us to use.

■ Our expectations of children's understanding need to be realistic and informed by developmental milestones and knowledge of the individual child.

■ Providing a rich learning environment includes thinking about opportunities for behavioural learning.

■ Planning processes are the same for behaviour as any other area of learning.

■ 'Can do' statements formulated from observations help to construct effective next steps.

■ Identifying adult actions increases the likelihood of giving children the best possible chance to achieve their next step.

■ Involving parents in discussions about behavioural learning from the start of your relationship helps to provide a shared understanding of any specific concerns which might arise.

The photocopiables that follow provide a possible format for recording 'can do' statements, next steps and adult actions – photocopy the sheets back to back.

| Child's name: | DOB: | |
|---|---|---|
| Date: | | |

| 'Can do' statements, from observation on: _____ (Note observable behaviour, context and length of time) _____ (child's first name) can: | Focus for next step (tick if yes) |
|---|---|
| | |
| | |
| | |
| | |
| | |
| | |
| | |
| | |
| Priorities for next step (change one element of 'can do' statement to make next step) _____ (child's first name) will: | Date achieved |
| 1 | |
| 2 | |
| 3 | |

Details of adult actions to support _____ to achieve next step

| Next step number | Adult action (prepare, prompt, practise, praise) | Impact: Very effective (VE) Effective (E) Not effective (NE) |
|---|---|---|
| | | |
| | | |
| | | |
| | | |
| | | |
| | | |
| | | |
| | | |
| | | |
| | | |
| | | |
| | | |
| | | |

# CHAPTER 6

# Social communication

The development of social competency is a very complex process of which language is a major part. We seldom take time to think about what skills, understanding and knowledge are needed to support our social communication. If we treat social communication in the same way as we treat other areas of the curriculum, then we can apply the same skills. This enables us to break down the learning for the child and focus on our role in finding ways to make the learning more manageable for each child.

From the information in Chapter 4 we can see that the development of language and communication is a very complex process. Babies are born with a predisposition to language which then develops as they mature. There are some predictable milestones which we would expect a child to experience but the age range for individual children will of course be variable.

The development of language is only a part of social communication. Once we start to put language in the context of social communication the process becomes considerably more complex. Each of us gives and receives messages and makes sense of the world around us in a variety of ways including:

- Facial expressions

- Body language

- Touch

- Spoken word

- Signs and gestures

- Intonation

- Visual images.

This is a very complex set of information which we are able to accept, process and make sense of before responding. We do it without thinking consciously much of the time. The fact that it is such a complex process obviously means that there is a range of things which might not progress as expected. This need not be an indication of a severe, long-term difficulty or disability.

**Going on a journey together**

What is important is that, as practitioners, we are able to use our observations and detailed next steps to evidence the child's individual progress. The observation would give the opportunity to compare responses to different contexts, people and activities. Our evidence gathering then enables us to look for patterns which can inform our planning.

As we have discussed in earlier chapters, it is essential to share the observation, assessment and planning process with parents and that they are able to contribute to it. This is particularly useful if we begin to see a pattern of observation which suggests that the child's skills and knowledge are not progressing as we would have expected.

In the area of communication, it is not just the ability to use language or signs to make our needs known but the willingness and desire to do so. A child may have all the skills and ability needed to communicate but no desire or willingness to do so. There can be many reasons for this, and, of course, it is dependent on the child's age and general developmental stage.

A child's personality – being quiet, shy, loud, extrovert and so on – will directly impact on their willingness and desire to interact with others. Previous experience is often difficult to gather information about but will make quite a difference to a child's reactions. In our current society it is common for children to experience group childcare from two years old, if not before. This is very different from a few years ago when, for most children, the first experience of group care was entry to school. Being one of a group in the shared care of a small number of adults makes significant demands on an individual's social understanding. The first social relationship a child develops is with their main carer. This relationship is initially focused on survival and the basic needs of food, warmth, safety. However, these needs are very hard to separate from the emotional element which provides the basis for communication, relationships and future learning. The quality of the first relationship provides a model which future relationships will add to and be compared with. This is not done consciously but we gradually build up a picture and expectations of what a relationship is and the part we play in its success. If in this first relationship we experience our needs being met appropriately, adequate amounts of attention and reciprocal communication, then our unconscious expectation would be that the next relationship would follow a similar pattern. To suddenly go from a small number of familiar, predictable relationships to a large number of new and unpredictable relationships can be a very scary experience for anyone, never mind a young child. If the new set of relationships are based on the same values and principles as those established at home, then the readjustments are less dramatic and mainly focus on finding our place in the new group. However, this is a difficult situation to create: we can only try to get as close to it as possible. The more we understand about the children and their families when youngsters first come to our setting, the more chance we have of understanding how complex they may find settling in to the culture of the setting.

The process of allocating a keyworker becomes extremely important and this relationship will be significant, especially in the first few weeks, in helping children feel safe and valued as they have done at home. From the adults' point of view it may be easier for each keyworker to have the same number of children allocated on a first come, first served basis. From the child's point of view it could make a huge difference if there was some thought given to matching personality and ethnicity, building on initial joint interest or experience. The role of keyworker needs to be clearly described and discussed so that all staff feel confident in their role when children first attend the setting and able to maintain the relationship when things are difficult as well as when they are going smoothly. The impact on the child of seeing significant adults working together harmoniously will be very positive and supportive.

It is likely that one of the strangest things to get used to, for children when they attend childcare settings, will be sharing adult time with so many other children. Although they will not have experienced exclusive attention all of the time, sharing with even three other children and the usual demands of daily life can be quite a shock. The first social need for the children, then, is to find an effective way to gain adult attention when they need it. If the culture of the setting is such that more of the phrases and interaction involving adults are about telling children what they should not be doing, then this is likely to give the message to children that most attention is given for inappropriate behaviour. This then becomes a vicious cycle with children using such behaviour to gain our attention and us giving more and more attention to the inappropriate behaviour. It is more effective to ensure that most comments and attention are directly focused on praising and telling children what it is they are doing which is appropriate and desirable. Once they have begun to establish a positive relationship with their keyworker, this then provides children with the basis for relationships with other adults and children. The keyworker role at this point is to ensure that other adults understand the ways in which the child communicates, comments and responds. This has a positive effect and can encourage the child to take part in activities with increased confidence. This also needs to happen in the process of establishing relationships with other children, with the adult mediating and interpreting intentions to support positive experiences for the majority of situations.

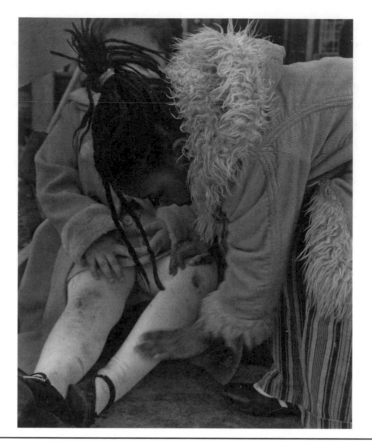

**Looking after each other**

'**Is it better to wear trousers at nursery?**'

Very quickly it will become apparent that some children, through their personality, temperament, previous experience or current supportive relationships, are able to manage their transition into the group situation with ease. As with every other area of learning, some children will find this considerably more difficult than others. From the practitioners' perspective understanding how difficult the settling time can be helps to provide a context which enables them to think about the child's social progress in the same way as other areas of learning. This focus on what the child 'can do' currently enables consideration of appropriate, achievable next steps with identifiable adult actions which will support the child's social learning.

Firstly, observations will give a clear picture of the child's current way of approaching others to make contact. This may range from hitting out to smiling and asking to play. The role of the adults is to consider the intention of the communication and to support the use of more appropriate ways of getting the child's message across or extending their current skill level. So, for example, if a child currently hits out, it is the role of the adults to look for the communication in this response. This should not be a random guess but a hypothesis based on the evidence contained in our observations. The observations need to be factual and relate to a variety of situations and times of day.

Although some strategies and small step learning will be focused on individual children, we also need to review the ways in which we are supporting the social learning for all children. As adults we often expect that children will gradually absorb the social expectations we and the group make. Increasingly, I feel we need to be more explicit about the learning which needs to take place and the ways in which we:

- introduce the ideas

- involve the children in deciding on appropriate social communication

- revisit and extend learning for all children.

**Looking after the babies together**

If we look at social communication in the same way as other areas of learning, these elements are part of the normal teaching and learning process. Our role is ensuring that whatever starting point children are currently at, we give them the best possible chance to achieve the next step in their learning.

Following a child's progress through the possible milestones set out in Table 6.1 gives us an opportunity to use our knowledge and understanding of individual children to support their learning and to think about what the next step might be. There are deliberately no age ranges included in this outline because the journey will take considerably longer for some children than others and the contextual influence will be significant. The contextual influence is just as significant for children as for adults, so we may feel relaxed and confident at home or shopping and be able to respond in a mature and socially competent way. However, at work we may feel more anxious or worried which would reduce our confidence and make it more difficult for us to respond in that same mature and socially competent way. Even if children seem to have a secure understanding of some of the social situations and responses they will be unable to use them appropriately on some occasions. This could either be because of the strength of emotion being experienced or the context in which the situation has occurred.

Although there are no age ranges or even a strict order to developing the understanding and social competencies described in Table 6.1, we will begin to build a picture of an individual child's progress through our observations. Undoubtedly, some children will appear to get stuck at a particular stage, just as they do in other areas of learning. It is our role to notice this and to find ways of helping their learning and experience to move on. If we notice such a situation and feel that the rate of progress is not as we would expect for a given child, as a first step it is important to share this concern with others. From a practitioner's perspective it is important to discuss concerns both with more experienced colleagues and with parents. As we gain professional experience we have a wider range of children and their different responses to use as an idea of what is likely or unlikely in terms of children's development. This range of experience needs to be constantly reviewed and challenged so that we don't slip into thinking that if we have met one child who responds in a particular way and was later diagnosed with a particular condition, that all children who respond in that way will have the same outcome. The process of diagnosis, especially in the area of social and communication abilities, is seldom straightforward – mainly because of the complex interaction of skills, understanding, experiences and abilities.

In order to be able to communicate we need to:

- have something to communicate
- be able to remember what we want to communicate
- be able to use a communication system to pass on the information
- be able to give the information meaning
- know if the message has been received by another
- be able to recognise the impact the message has had on another.

This is a tall order when you begin to think about it in terms of a young child's learning capacity and understanding. We will gradually learn through our observations that particular children are finding elements of this process very difficult. For example:

- being able to hold on to what they want to say for long enough to organise their communication system

- being able to generate their own independent thinking rather than using repeated phrases provided by others

- needing to repeat a message several times because they are unclear if it has been received

- struggling to identify the impact their communication has had so increasing the strength with which it is delivered, e.g. shouting, changing tone, physical gestures, etc.

- coping with increased anxiety or emotion while trying to deliver their message

- being able to take sufficient time to communicate what they want others to know

- coping with another's full attention while they try to collect their thoughts and communicate their message

- tune out other things which are going on around them while they concentrate on their communication.

All of these suggestions may well be indicators of a particular condition, syndrome or disability but they are also common stages and difficulties which children and adults experience in their daily communication with others. There is a healthy balance which can be struck between supporting individual learning and awareness of current difficulty with anxiety about possible longer-term concerns and possible future diagnosis. This balance can best be achieved through sharing concerns with parents and colleagues in a professional way and firmly based on observation-based evidence. If the concern goes on for longer than would be anticipated by all the adults involved, then the next step is to seek advice from other professionals. The evidence which has been collected in the form of observations which provide information about:

- the learning opportunities

- rate of progress

- strategies used

- indication of why this issue is causing concern

- adult action and strategies which have been tried

will give other professionals a clear picture of what can be tried next to support the child's learning. Although sometimes practitioners and parents can feel it is important to gain a diagnosis of some kind, this in itself will not make any difference to the child's responses. The diagnosis has more impact on the adult understanding of the child and gives a justification for why the child may be having difficulty. While I agree there are some times when a diagnosis is helpful in guiding future thinking, I believe that through focusing on providing the best possible chance for learning which is based on sound knowledge and understanding of the child we are most likely to really help the child to overcome any current difficulties. We are learning companions and have the role of being an advocate for all children even if sometimes we find their responses difficult to deal with ourselves.

**Key points**

- Language development is complex and forms one part of the development of social communication skills.

- As adults we often struggle with social competence and different contexts can make it either easier or harder for us.

- We seldom share our social communication skills in a professional way with children to support their learning.

- Although each individual child will learn at a different rate and in a different way we can identify some key skills and stages in learning.

- Once the stages have been identified we can be clear about the type of support we can give to provide children with the best possible chance of developing social competence.

- Some of the difficulties which children experience may well be indicators of more long-term needs and possibly even a future diagnosis of a condition or disability.

- Our role is to gather factual evidence through our observations of the child's response to learning activities and day-to-day situations. We need to do this from the perspective of the child's best interests without our own value judgements.

The photocopiables that follow provide a possible format for recording observation notes, further action and contact with other agencies.

**Table 6.1 Helping children to meet developmental milestones in social communication**

| Child activity | Adult support |
| --- | --- |
| Responding to adult smiles, cooing, etc. | Frequent engagement in reciprocal communication, imitating child's actions and sounds. Try to identify toys, objects, people who generate positive response |
| Imitating facial expression and noises | Develop 'conversation' with turn taking for brief spells, e.g. two turns of surprise response |
| Initiating sound imitation with some turn taking | Use games and rhymes (e.g. round and round the garden, peekaboo), to encourage longer turn taking and higher interest levels. Change turn taking by holding child's hand to do round and round the garden on your hand |
| Beginning to use sounds to attract attention, maintain contact with another | Encourage positive communication between children both the same age and older. Interpret sounds and signals for both children, e.g. 'You're looking away now; I think you've had enough of this game now'. Use explanation to help children understand their own and others' possible feelings. Use lots of rhymes, action and rhythm games to enable children to build and reinforce relationships with each other |
| Using a variety of methods to gain attention from others including verbal, physical and facial expressions | Use predictable phrases to ask children to play. Through observation make a collection of words children in the setting use to indicate they would like to play. Use these as the basis of your modelling and suggestions. Give lots of praise when you hear the phrases being used. Give clear, simple message that we should talk first. If physical activity develops into hurting, give clear messages that this is not acceptable but think about what is being communicated and encourage a different way of expressing. Reflect back to children how you think they might be feeling and why you think that, e.g. 'Your eyebrows are very crinkled; I think you might be feeling cross' before trying to find out or suggest why |
| Some conflict occurs relating to wanting own way, a particular toy or frustration about not being able to do something | Use a predictable process for resolving conflict. Encourage children to be involved in deciding the solution and make all the thinking explicit: 'I think that might have made you feel sad if Joey broke your model'. Interpret any communication the child might offer. 'I hate you', for example, is often used to communicate just how much a child wants something so the reframing could be 'You really wanted to go on the bike very much'. Use stories and role-play situations to enable children to practise without feeling the strength of emotion |
| Finding communication which will enable joining a game | Highlight the words/phrases which are currently being used in the setting for children to indicate they would like to join in. Praise children who use the phrases and those who let the child join in the game/activity. Model the phrases when you ask children to join you for an activity. Encourage children to find as many different ways of asking as possible. Use stories, puppets and role play to explore the possible scenarios |
| Finding communication which will maintain a relationship for the length of the game | Listen for things children currently say to each other during anactivity. These phrases are important to build connections between those involved. These are the phrases which no matter what words are used give the message that 'it would be good to play with you again'. Model some phrases when you are involved in an activity with a group of children, e.g. 'That was kind when you gave the dice to Shamina. You are doing well, Alesha, you have five teddies already' etc. |

▶

**Table 6.1** *Continued*

| | |
|---|---|
| Finding acceptable ways of saying they don't want to play | Identify phrases which children can use to say they do not wish to play. Highlight the phrases with the whole group. Clarify with all children that it is OK to say they do not want to play sometimes. Talk about the fact that this just means that you don't want to play this game now, not that you never want to play or that you will never be friends with the person asking you to play. Praise appropriate use of phrases, exploring possible reasons why someone might not want to play, e.g. feeling tired, sad, excited about something else, involved in another activity, don't like the game, want to be inside/outside at the moment, etc. Use stories, puppets and role play to explore the possibilities |
| Finding acceptable ways of expressing anger, sadness, fear, excitement, frustration, etc. | This is one of the hardest things for children to begin to understand. Adults have very high expectations of children which they cannot always fulfil themselves! Make sure the message you give is that it is OK to feel any of these emotions and that there are different ways of expressing them. Help children to explore what kind of things make them feel each of the emotions. Make a collection of different ways in which these could be expressed appropriately. Remember that when we feel any strong emotion our thinking skills are hijacked and we are not able to think through all the consequences of our actions. Discuss with colleagues what will be considered acceptable expression of some of the feelings and the ways in which we will encourage children to try responding that way. There may be particular areas of the room which children can use to have a little time away from a difficult situation. Be realistic in your expectations of individual children: think of the last time you were angry; were you able to calmly tell a grownup what was wrong? Use stories, puppets and role play to explore the possibilities |
| Finding acceptable ways to ask for help | Collect observations of when individual children have indicated that they need help. Use an appropriate word or phrase which they can begin to use to get help. Ensure that all adults know about and respond appropriately to both the indication and the phrase. Add the word or phrase to a collection which the children suggest and are used regularly in the group. These will start off as one word and gradually build to 2- or 3-word phrases |
| Recognising own feelings | Use mirrors, pictures of facial expressions, stories, puppets to extend children's awareness of the variety of expressions and possible feelings which might be linked with them. From observations identify signals which children give to indicate how they are feeling, e.g. change in facial expression, body language, going to a particular area of the room, going to a particular adult or child |
| Recognising feelings of others | As above, but exploring how different characters in a story might feel about one situation. Use real situations and photographs to talk about how someone might feel then check out with them if the suggestion was accurate. Encourage children to suggest a variety of feelings; there is no right or wrong answer no matter how obvious it might look to us! Value each response without making a judgement about its accuracy. Give the clear message that in a slightly different situation the child may well have felt like that. It is important that we help children to understand that people have different feelings about the same situation but that we can get clues about how they might be feeling |
| Helping other children if hurt or wanting a particular toy | These tend to be just occasional events to start with but if we can praise and talk through the feelings which each child could have experienced, then we are most likely to increase the frequency of it happening. Role model appropriate ways to offer and receive help. Remember, sometimes children don't want to be helped and we jump in a bit too quickly |
| Initiating and maintaining relationships with other children and adults, including being able to resolve conflicts or differences of opinion | Gradually children begin to piece together previous experience to work towards this ideal. However, as very few of us as adults can achieve this consistently, it is a totally unrealistic expectation of young children! |

## Observation notes

Child's name:                          DOB:

Date:

Context: Where? What activity? Time of day? Who with (adults and children)?

| Time | What I saw |
|------|------------|
|      |            |

## Notes from discussion about observation

Child's name:                                    DOB:

Observation date:

Discussion date:

Those involved in discussion:

| Things noted from observation (learning opportunities offered, rate of progress in learning, response to adult strategy, indication of concern) | Action to be taken | Impact of action and date completed |
|---|---|---|
|  |  |  |
|  |  |  |
|  |  |  |
|  |  |  |
|  |  |  |
|  |  |  |
|  |  |  |
|  |  |  |
|  |  |  |
|  |  |  |
|  |  |  |
|  |  |  |
|  |  |  |
|  |  |  |

## Following up concerns and contacting other agencies

Child's name:                                    DOB:

| Concern (from observation discussion date _____ ) | Shared with (contact name and title, e.g. Health visitor etc.) | Date |
|---|---|---|
|  |  |  |
|  |  |  |
|  |  |  |
|  |  |  |

Completed by:

# Able and talented

It is tempting to focus on offering learning opportunities which are related to the child's area of ability in a narrow or closed way. Offering open-ended problem-solving opportunities enables children to deepen and broaden their learning. Our good practice of observation, assessment and planning for individual learning is crucial in supporting children who are able and talented. There can be significant challenges for adults working with children who ask questions we can't answer. Sharing understanding of the child's learning with parents provides the opportunity to combine the advantages of both environments to foster the child's particular talent and general learning.

**We all have such a lot to learn from each other**

Usually, when we think about children with special educational needs (SEN), we focus on those for whom there are barriers to learning and achievement. Children, in the early years, who are able and talented often present as being able to learn quickly and make links between their learning with ease. We are all very aware that all children learn skills and concepts at different rates and often in different ways. This rate of progress is seldom consistent and sometimes seems to slow right down for a short spell. To make things more complicated this is true of each separate area of learning. It is all the more important to ensure that we collect a broad range of observations to evidence a child's current learning across different areas of the curriculum. For most children we know there are skills, activities and situations which they find easier than others. In our observations and next step planning we need to take account of this knowledge to extend the opportunities we offer to children to support their learning. It is very tempting to provide more of the things that they can do, or to move to more formal learning such as worksheets of numbers, letters, addition sums. We tend to do this, I think, because we feel that this will prepare them for what we assume will be on offer at school. However, it is more helpful if we use the knowledge and experience we have gained about how children learn and the role we play in that process. Rather than narrowing the learning opportunities to worksheet or more formal activities it is more effective to try to broaden the opportunities on offer.

The crucial information which we need is the evidence from our observations. This provides us with detailed information which can help us plan activities and opportunities which children are likely to engage in and find challenging. Our observations need to provide a range of information about each child. For example, in what way do the children prefer to be involved with their learning?

- Hearing about it from an adult or child first.

- Watching others doing it first.

- Trying it out themselves then talking about it with others.

- Seeing what others have done in pictures or photographs before attempting anything themselves.

From our observations we can begin to build a detailed picture of the child's preferred approach to a new activity and this will give us some indication of the learning style which they find most helpful. Most of us use a variety of learning styles in different situations, but if presented with a difficult new piece of learning, we would be likely to have a preference regarding the way it was introduced. This will be mainly one of the following:

- Visual – through pictures, diagrams, etc.

- Auditory – hearing sounds or words.

- Kinaesthetic – involving movement and action.

It is then possible to link this information with the signals we see which tell us that the child is really involved in their current activity. For example, a child who is totally involved in an activity will not be easily distracted by what is going on around them; they may tend to stand or sit in a particular way, have a particular facial expression and ways of moving. By identifying these clearly and looking for them during our observations we can build an evidenced picture of the child's learning style and the activities which they tend to be most involved in. Providing a balance of child-initiated and adult-initiated activities contributes to our understanding of the things which particularly interest and motivate the child. The gathering of this detailed information is of course important for all children but can be especially useful when it comes to children who show signs of being more able. It could be tempting to spend less time observing and looking at the evidence we gather for children whose learning progresses almost in spite of us. However, the Every Child Matters agenda and the Office for Standards in Education (Ofsted) framework help to focus our minds on 'What is the child's experience of being in this setting?' Thinking about this, both from the perspective of one day's experience as well as over longer periods of time, can help us to look at what we are offering each child. The purpose of the Ofsted question and the situation we are developing is that, through the opportunities and environment, we offer each child an experience of purposeful, active learning on a daily basis. Our own evaluation of the day should include reflection on how effective our organisation and interactions have been in facilitating individual children's learning.

In building up our knowledge and evidence of individual children's learning patterns we can begin to see which areas of learning are their strengths and which are developing more slowly. This overall pattern can highlight areas of particular ability and talent. It may be that a child's overall learning pattern shows a balance of high achievement across all areas of the curriculum or that there are specific areas which show high achievement and understanding. The pattern across different areas of learning is important because it can have an impact on the social interactions which a child develops and the learning opportunities we offer.

For a child who has a particular area of learning which they understand more readily than their peers, the communication with those peers can be problematic. From the child's perspective, their thinking is far ahead of the other children and their level of understanding, providing self-motivation to discover new things. For young children, their level of maturity and experience would be unlikely to enable them to patiently help another child towards understanding what they find easy. This can develop a sense of frustration but also a feeling of being different and possibly isolated. The response of the adult is crucial in protecting both the child's individual level of knowledge and the other children's developing understanding. The other important factor is to consider the impact on the self-esteem of the children.

As individuals we need to feel competent, accepted and valued by those around us, particularly those who are important to us. As adults, trying to keep up with a child who has particular talent can be very challenging and can contribute to us not feeling competent. This can, in turn, make us feel irritated with the child involved.

But it is important to look at challenging their problem solving and conceptual understanding rather than just repeating what we know they can already do. For example, children who particularly like playing with numbers and find it easy to collect specific numbers of objects, find numerals, even combine groups of numbers don't need endless practice of these skills. They need opportunities to apply their skills to real situations and to explore problems which involve numbers in their solution.

Providing a worksheet for them to complete will not provide an opportunity for the development of this creative and complex type of thinking. Giving children breadth of experience and variety of experiences to explore and add to their conceptual thinking ensures that they are able

**Problem solving**

to apply their knowledge and skills when appropriate. For example, combining a child's interest in cars with their ability with number could result in an activity related to finding a way of comparing how fast or how far the cars can travel relative to each other. In the first instance, the child may try working with a friend and pushing the cars along the floor. This provides the opportunity to talk with the children about:

- how to record how far they have travelled

- whether or not it is always the same

- what happens if different children push the cars

- how the amount of push could be the same for all cars

- what would happen if we wanted to compare five cars at the same time

- what would happen if this was done on a different surface

- how you could explain to someone else how to repeat the comparison between the cars.

It would be much quicker for the adult to provide two cars and to tell the children how to enable both cars to start 'fairly', letting go rather than pushing them. The amount of learning and understanding on the child's part would be considerably reduced. It is the posing of questions, particularly the 'What if …?' questions, which provide support for children to focus their thinking and problem-solving skills. The process of trying out possible ideas, sharing suggestions with other children and using the things that go wrong to build the next solution is what makes the activity so much richer than just getting it 'right'. In some cases this can be very challenging for the adults providing this learning activity. Mainly this is when the children begin to explore ideas that we would never have thought of at their age or in some cases even now as adults. As adults our experience of learning is of course very different from the children we are working with today. For many of us, we remember most clearly our secondary schooling, which is generally more formally based than the children in our settings are likely to experience. The curriculum offered in our schools has broadened and deepened since we were involved in it, even if this was only a year ago! The nature of knowledge and understanding is that it continues to increase and expand because we are always building on the work others have done before us. We cannot unknow things which are known. This means that the learning which we were involved in at secondary school, for example understanding which foods are healthy and nutritious, is now being explored at a much earlier age and stage. The children we are working with now will be the adults who extend the knowledge, understanding and conceptual boundaries that are currently in place.

In some cases working with children who are likely to be able and talented can be quite a threatening and deskilling experience. Frequently the child will be able to formulate questions which we would never have thought of, or know the answer to. In a situation where we usually have the position of holding most knowledge, this can feel quite uncomfortable. The important thing to consider is the way in which we respond to those challenging questions. Our priority needs to be to encourage and support children's learning and discovery at their level. To do this effectively we need to value their questions, knowledge and understanding by responding positively and enabling them to explore ways of extending their learning. To take the role of learning companion and to encourage children's exploration through our own questioning and prompting can be a really valuable experience for children. We can focus our own responses and questions on encouraging more exploration which helps children take another step on their learning journey.

Without doubt there will also be frustrations for the children themselves, which can be related to a variety of issues. Likely areas which can result in feelings of frustration are:

- thinking/working faster than physical ability

- thinking/working faster than language ability

- others not understanding what you mean

- finding the vocabulary to describe what you can visualise

- finding the equipment/tools which will do what you need

- not being taken seriously

- others thinking you are 'only playing' when you are trying to work something out

### Exploring

- others not wanting to spend time with you because they see you as being much 'cleverer' than them

- being teased and made fun of because you get so involved in a particular area of interest

- feeling reluctant to engage in activities that you are not so able to do.

As adults we often make assumptions about children's learning and understanding and it is particularly important, where a child presents as able and talented, that we understand that this level of ability may not extend to all areas of learning. It is our role to explore ways of increasing the child's confidence in areas which they find more challenging. This may include identifying ways to sensitively use their areas of strength and ways of problem solving to apply to other learning. One of the great challenges for all children is often social and emotional understanding and developing positive friendships with others. This can be particularly difficult if you are viewed as having knowledge and understanding which others do not share. It reduces the opportunity for equal shared conversation about tasks because one child has so much more understanding but lacks the maturity to be able to engage another child sensitively in joint learning. Clearly the adult has a role in mediating between children and providing a bridge between the different levels of understanding so that it does not adversely affect either self-esteem or social connection between the children.

The same good practice suggestions about sharing the learning journey with parents applies where children display particular areas of ability and talent. A particularly useful way of recording and sharing the child's experiences is to use photographs with your observations and annotations of the learning which has taken place. Children themselves are likely to find using a camera very helpful, and quick, to record their activities. These photographs can be compiled into books so that both adults and children can revisit previous learning, share ideas with others and review their own thinking process.

In the same way that we, as practitioners, may feel challenged by able children and have to think carefully about the learning activities we offer, parents may often have concerns about whether their child is getting the best opportunities. Particularly with younger children, there may be a temptation to think that the best approach is to concentrate only on the child's area of talent in the belief that they will be able to develop their other learning once they are older. This would have most impact in the realm of social and emotional understanding and developing relationships with other children of a similar age. Often, able children will find it easier to relate to older children and adults. However, being able to initiate and establish relationships is something which we need to explore as a developmental process. Generally, we are more able to be tolerant of those younger than us. If we are developing relationships only with those older than us, we will be less likely to need to learn about the impact of our own behaviour on the relationship. Any interaction is a combination of the behaviour and response of each person involved. Under the umbrella of 'behaviour' is included the facial expression, body language, tone of voice, personal space and understanding of the person. These are complex things to learn about and yet we all use them constantly every day. We have learned about them mainly through trial and error from those younger, older, and the same age as ourselves. The balance is important, as is the support from adults when difficulties occur. It is a major part of the adults' role in an early years setting to understand and plan for the developing social understanding of all children who attend.

Through our process of observation and assessment and identifying next steps for children's learning, we do need to consider what we would see which would lead us to think a child might be able or talented. We can be easily led into very stereotypical approaches in our thinking and to only consider specific areas of the curriculum as possible areas of special ability. The key factors which would highlight a child's particular ability will be the same for all areas of learning and all children: namely, level of involvement, evidence of independent understanding, application of learning, evidence of conceptual knowledge and rate of progress. We probably feel relatively confident in thinking about these elements in relation to musical, numerical and language ability, but we can support children best if we extend our thinking to other areas of the curriculum. For example, some children may develop a particularly scientific approach to their learning which is evidenced both through their developing understanding in the area of Knowledge and Understanding of the World and in their way of tackling new learning. Perhaps they are particularly able to gather detailed information, use previous learning and logically apply this to the new situation and produce original ways of solving the problems presented. In Creative Development, certain children may develop very comprehensive understanding of different materials and ways to combine them to express themselves with originality. Probably the most unlikely areas for us to consider as a particular ability would be Personal, Social and Emotional learning. However, being able to recognise, express and learn about your own emotions and the feelings of others appropriately is a set of skills which can play a major part in children's future lives.

The key thing about identifying areas in which individual children are particularly able is not about labelling but about ensuring that we are supporting and planning for the child's learning appropriately. Using our evidence of observation, work samples and photographs we can share our understanding of the child's learning both with parents and colleagues with a view to finding appropriately challenging activities. In the first instance our discussions would be restricted to colleagues in our setting. However, advice can also be requested from local support teams.

Sometimes we are reluctant to seek advice for children who are progressing really well, but it is just as important to be certain that we are meeting their needs in the same way as other children in our care. The Area SENCO and Local Authority support teams will be able to provide local advice about other services and groups which could be accessed. The Internet can be particularly useful in accessing information to support children who are able, talented or gifted. It is essential that we use our professional knowledge and experience to be selective in judging the quality and appropriateness of the information and suggestions. Just because it is on a website, in a book, or on television does not immediately make it the best quality information available to meet our current need. If in doubt, compare information from several sources and check it out with one of the support teams before implementing the suggestions.

 **Key points**

- Good practice in the observation, assessment and planning process is essential to meet individual children's learning needs.

- Children who are able and talented are best supported through broadening their thinking about their particular area of ability rather than formal or restrictive activities such as a worksheet-based activity.

- The role of the adult is to support further exploration through appropriate and sensitive open-ended questioning such as:

  - What would happen if …?

  - What would it be like if …?

  - How could we …?

  - What would we see if …?

  - What do you think we could use to …?

- Relationships between able children and their peers can be problematic as a result of misunderstanding and frustration.

- Advice and support is available from local SEN support teams.

- Information is available on the Internet but be wary of the quality of the suggestions. Use professional judgement, compare information from a variety of sources and check with support teams.

## Able and talented observation: things to think about

- Describe the facial expressions and body language of the child which tells you they are involved in an activity or interaction.

- Describe first signs of anxiety, frustration, conflict (this could be changes in facial expression, body language, etc.).

- Describe approaches to learning opportunities: does the child look first, have a go, watch someone else, look at pictures or instructions first?

- Notice particular materials the child likes to use (mobilo, clay, collage, bricks, etc.).

- Identify children who work well together when this child is in the group.

- Identify particular areas of interest. Ask parents for information about interests shown at home.

- Notice the balance of the child's day, particularly time spent:

  - alone or with others

  - inside or outside

  - physically active or sitting at an activity

  - involved in favourite activity or other activities

  - with adults or with children

  - with own age range or older/younger.

- Identify opportunities for the child to make autonomous decisions about the order in which they do things, where they do them, with whom and for how long, without being singled out or being treated differently.

- Make a collection of open-ended questions which staff can use to encourage further exploration and enquiry, such as:

  - What if ... you made it taller/wider/there were no more bricks to use?

  - What would happen if ... you used the sand and the glue together/the giant wanted to live in the house you have made?

  - Could you find a way to ... make it stronger/faster/move five dolls across the room?

- Ensure that activities can be continued the following day, models added to, imaginative play developed further, unusual items are available to be included and to stimulate further problem solving.

- Identify opportunities to play alongside the child to support social connections and reduce frustration by adding explanation and suggestions to other children who are playing.

- Provide creative 'surprises' to be found which stimulate the imagination, such as something landing from space in the outdoor area, letters from someone in another nursery, a letter from one of the teddies about his adventures.

- Use photographs and book making to record achievements so that they can be revisited.

- Let children take their own photographs to communicate with others about things they like/don't like, things they have enjoyed, people they like to be with.

The final photocopiable offers a possible format to record the link between an observation, the development activity and the child's response.

## Discussion of observation notes

Child's name:                                     DOB:

Observation date:

Date of discussion:

| Area of interest from observation notes | Suggestion for development | Child's response (dated) |
|---|---|---|
| | | |
| | | |
| | | |
| | | |

Completed by:

# CHAPTER 8

# Medical diagnosis

There are increasing numbers of children with a diagnosis or medical needs in our settings. Our attitude can make or break the relationship with parents and child. Our anxieties can best be addressed through prioritising and problem solving with parents. These anxieties are often related to lack of knowledge or experience. Working with other professionals can effectively support the child, parents and practitioners. Diagnosis related to behaviour can be the most challenging in terms of adult attitudes and supporting parents. Your relationship with parents can be a central driver in your journey towards continuous improvement.

Anyone working in childcare today will be aware of the importance of developing and improving our inclusive practice. Increasingly, children with medical needs and a range of disabilities are able to attend their local childcare setting. This is true whether it is a day nursery, preschool, children's centre or childminder. The Disability Discrimination Act is the legislation which has significantly impacted on our awareness of the need to make our settings more inclusive. This idea of an inclusive setting can be very challenging. We can all currently, I suspect, bring to mind a disability or medical need which we feel we would be unable to accommodate in our setting. In my experience the real barrier to including children is our own attitude to their presence and our lack of knowledge about the individual child's needs. We have an opportunity, in early years settings, to lead and celebrate the moves towards all children and adults being included in our society in the future. The benefits for all our children of learning together, sharing experiences and learning about each other as individuals are invaluable. The challenge is for the adults to learn to be as inclusive in their attitude as the children. Without doubt the children will take their lead from us while they are in our setting. Our role modelling needs to exemplify the messages we would like to convey about our values and principles. Currently these messages are likely to include our aim to:

- value

- respect

- care for

- keep safe

those who are involved in our setting. In this context we cannot then start to pick and choose who we will treat in this way.

**Learning about each other**

The main basis for our anxiety as practitioners is usually related to lack of information, knowledge and therefore fear of the unknown situations which may arise. Often through getting to know families and the specific needs of individual children we can begin to work together to consider the problems and difficulties which might arise and ways in which we can resolve them. Our initial meeting with parents is our first opportunity to give the messages listed. It is therefore worth exploring our current practice to identify ways to improve that first contact experience. Asking current and previous parents involved with us for their views increases the likelihood of our improvements being in line with what parents would really find helpful.

Although the main role of our setting is to provide childcare we are also likely to be a focus for the local community especially those with young children. We are able to provide role modelling and a positive experience for many families and will often become a first port of call for advice and information. The way in which we respond will influence what people believe about us and those involved with us. If we are proactive in our messages of welcoming, respecting and valuing all families, then it is more likely that the environment in our setting will develop into one in which everyone feels safe both emotionally and physically. In being explicit about the ways in which we relate to each other, we can support all adults and children in our setting community to be respectful of each other too.

The journey of getting to know your child is a complex, exciting and emotional experience for most parents. The balance between these different feelings will usually depend on your own personality, the family and friend support network you have and the professionals you meet on your journey. If your child has particular medical needs or a diagnosis at birth, your journey will immediately have more professionals involved in your child's life. It is impossible to understand how a particular parent feels in this situation as there are so many factors which will impact on their response. The variety of responses are likely to include, at some stage, some or all of the following emotions:

- Joy

- Happiness

- Anger

- Fear

- Anxiety

- Frustration

- Helplessness

- Isolation.

Each parent and each family's experience will be different so we cannot have a standard response which assumes that they are experiencing any particular emotion. The fact that a child has a particular medical need, diagnosis or disability does not mean that we need to respond any differently when the parent arrives at our setting. Each and every parent will want to be:

- welcomed for who they are, not what you think they should be

- listened to in a respectful way

- convinced that you will welcome and support their child

- provided with accurate and appropriate information.

At the introductory meeting you will probably be unaware of exactly what you may need to do to support the child, but this is true of any initial visit. The problem is that because you know there is an identified need you begin to feel anxious and worried that the situation will be too much for you or your staff to manage. If this is communicated to other adults, especially the parent who is visiting, the relationship is likely to be adversely affected from the beginning. If the relationship starts in such a doubtful way, it will take a lot of hard work to make up the lost ground.

The practical aspects of ensuring that the parent feels at ease in your setting and that the child settles well are the same as for any child. Good practice would suggest that you would provide at least the following information:

- The way in which your setting is organised.

- The activities which are available for children.

- The ways in which adults in the setting support children's learning.

- The way in which learning opportunities are planned to meet individual needs.

You would also try to gain the following information:

- Basic details: name, address, etc.

- Siblings.

- Child's previous experiences.

- Special toy, comforter.

- Child's likes and dislikes.

- Favourite foods, drinks.

- Ways the child will communicate requirements or parents' views of needs, e.g. hunger, toileting, needing comfort, preferred ways of being comforted, etc.

- Medication or particular health concerns.

This information gathering is all part of the establishment of the relationship between you. However, the balance of the discussion can be distorted if the information explored focuses more on the child's medical concerns than their personality and individuality. If the parents have had to cope with several professionals being involved prior to meeting you, then it is also likely that they will have had to tell their story many times in considerable detail to many people. The Early Support Programme (ESP) materials were designed to support parents of children with disabilities. Further information is available on the website www.earlysupport.org.uk. The materials were developed in consultation with parents and aim to reduce the need for parents to repeatedly tell their story or be the sole co-ordinator of the involvement of a variety of professionals. The Early Support Programme family pack provides information about the relevant medical issues for the child and a booklet for parents to complete, which tells the sequence of events and milestones which have occurred so far. The family packs are usually distributed by health professionals or early intervention teams such as Portage to families whose children are identified as having disabilities in the age range birth to three.

Although not all families who come to your setting will have the pack, it is worth reviewing your initial discussions with parents to maintain an appropriate balance between information about any special needs the child may have and your focus on abilities and interests. One of the issues which was raised through the development of the ESP materials was that it could be very difficult for families to access support if there was not specific diagnosis but a combination of agreed concerns. The family pack also provides a booklet of information which tries to support and provide information for families in this situation.

The principle which is central to developing good practice in working with children with disabilities and medical needs is the same as for any child. Evidence-based information about current achievements and effective use of next steps are used to provide access to a rich learning environment supported with high quality interactions with adults.

The first step in making this a reality is to learn about children as individuals and as members of their family. Working in partnership with adults at home can then provide the basis for joint problem solving.

When we think about a child with medical needs attending our setting, we often focus first on the medical need. This, I suppose, is partly because it is often a new situation for us, but also because our confidence in dealing with anything medical is often less than dealing with care and learning. The reality, though, is that if we take each problem and work through possible solutions, it becomes more manageable. For most of the practical situations in coping with mobility, administering medication and identifying priorities in particular situations, parents will have a vast amount of experience which they can draw on to help you. Providing the opportunity for the parent to spend some time with you in the setting, identifying potential barriers and taking part in discussions about risk assessment, can be very productive if approached sensitively.

The concept of risk and risk assessment is often new and, of course, worrying for parents when it is in relation to their child. Sometimes there can be difficulties in finding some common ground about situations where it is appropriate for children to experience and learn about risk and others where it would not be appropriate. Thinking about this from the parents' point of view, it is possible that they are feeling that their child is particularly vulnerable at this time when they are considering leaving them in the care of unfamiliar adults for extended periods. This can be an even stronger feeling if their child has needed extensive time in hospital or spent time in special care units at birth. While it is important to be realistic about the risks which exist, the dialogue needs to focus on the immediate priorities; other issues such as outings etc. can be reviewed once the child has settled and everyone is feeling a little more confident. The ideal is to plan the settling process in detail, considering:

- visits from parents to discuss the child starting at the setting

- visits from child and parent for a short period of time to familiarise themselves with the environment and people

- short sessions for the child without the parent

- parent role modelling nappy changing or toileting for staff so that the child feels at ease

- parent role modelling administration of medication

- dates to review how the process is going and if any adjustments are needed such as increasing the number of sessions/days because the child is settling well.

In fact, these are basically the same considerations you would have for any child. Regarding the medication it is essential that parents are informed of setting policy and procedure regarding administering medication. This should include arrangements for staff training – both basic background knowledge about the medication and training from the health professional involved with the individual child. Only the staff who have received both types of training should be involved in the actual administration of medication. Written documentation and training should include clear descriptions of when medication should be given, how much and what the consequences are if too much is given. Necessary arrangements for emergency situations should be explicitly discussed and agreed with parents and shared with all staff. A helpful and informative resource is *Including Me: Managing Complex Health Needs in Schools and Early Years Settings* written by Jeanne Carlin (2005) and available from the Council for Disabled Children and the National Children's Bureau. This book provides practical help, advice and information about many of the apparent difficulties and how they can be overcome.

In the same way that parents have had to be involved with a variety of professionals supporting them, it is likely that the same will be true for you when it is confirmed that the child will attend your setting. The key thing to remember is that all the adults involved will be trying to give the child the best possible chance of succeeding, but sometimes the priorities are different from different perspectives. The more the adults are able to discuss together at the same time

**Finding ways for us all to join in**

what the issues are, the more effectively the problems can be overcome. If you have a particular issue which needs to be discussed, rather than talking to several professionals individually, try to get them together so that they can each hear all the advice and concerns. This way of working and regularly reviewing the situation reduces the misunderstandings and focuses everyone's energies on the current priority for the child and family. From your perspective the chances of an effective and workable solution being discovered are vastly increased.

Of the disabilities and medical needs which you are likely to include in your setting, the ones which raise the anxiety levels most are where conditions are life-shortening, require oxygen regularly or are behaviour related. Where conditions are life-shortening it is important to ensure that families are able to access appropriate support services and that they feel able to do this at the necessary times. It may be that your role is as a facilitator – making this contact with the parents' consent. It is also essential that support is identified for the staff and consideration given to what information will be shared with other children and families. These discussions need to be sensitively handled with the child's parents and the other professionals involved.

There has recently been a significant increase in the number of children diagnosed and in some cases receiving medication to help them cope with Attention Deficit Hyperactivity Disorder (ADHD). One of the difficulties for adults supporting children with ADHD is that it confuses our personal views about dealing with behavioural issues. When we see a child behave in a particular way, we often make a judgement about how consciously the actions are carried out and whether the child 'knows what they are doing'. The difficulty with such judgements in relation to ADHD is that the child may well have an awareness of what they are doing and may well be repeating a previous behaviour, but their struggle is in finding a way to control what they are doing. This sounds so simple and we can think of situations which we ourselves are involved in where we think through the consequences, then make the decision not to respond in a particular way. This is really a very complex process of thinking and suppressing impulsive actions. Although it has taken us most of our lives to develop this ability there are, I'm sure, still situations where we are unable to have that level of control. For those with ADHD they are constantly struggling to gain or regain that ability to take time to consider the impact of an action before they do it. This must make daily life an unpredictable place.

Put simply the function of prescribed medication for this condition is to help to prioritise the sensory information being processed to enable thinking to have a more effective impact on actions. The medication is by no means a magic answer and it is important that behavioural learning opportunities are carefully thought through, consistent and supportive of the child's age, stage and ability. As with other conditions it is essential that advice is sought from the other professionals working with the child and family. There are many confusing elements in the diagnosis of this condition, for example:

- the extent of the difficulty

- previous behavioural experience of the child

- because the presenting difficulty is behavioural, other reasons for the behaviour may need to be explored

- descriptions of the behaviour may vary depending on who is describing and the context being reported.

It is important to remember that ADHD is a medical diagnosis and not a description of the way a child behaves and should not be used as such. Also there are many possible reasons for a child being very active, particularly in an early years setting including excitement or anxiety; our observations over time will be useful to develop an evidence-based description of the child's responses. It is particularly important to evidence explicitly our strategies for supporting children's behavioural learning, showing how we have differentiated the learning to meet the child's needs. Some of the suggestions in the section about behavioural learning (Chapter 5) may be helpful.

So far we have discussed the situation where children already have a diagnosis or their needs have been clearly identified and there are other professionals involved before they attend your setting. For most of us, this is a much more straightforward situation than when we are first to identify concerns about a child's development and progress. A major factor in this process is also whether or not all the adults involved agree on what the concerns are and the extent to which we need to intervene.

Bearing in mind our considerations at the beginning of the chapter and the variety of responses there may be to the recognition of the extent of a child's needs, our sensitivity is essential. As well as the good practice described in Chapter 3, relating to 'Sharing the learning journey with parents', we need to reflect on our own and the staff group's views about the child's needs and the parents' perspective. This is not about making judgements about a parent being 'in denial' or not recognising a problem which is obvious to us. It is much more about us reflecting on why there is a difference in views. As practitioners we are able to have a comparative view of a child's development. We have seen many children at this stage of their lives and we can be confident in our thinking about developmental milestones and roughly when a child may reach them. We have seen a variety of ways of supporting children who have needed additional help to progress. We have probably had positive experiences in our involvement with other professionals and seen how working together can be very effective in supporting the child. Seldom will parents have had a similar quantity of experience.

Apart from all of these considerations the ultimate one is that our relationship with the child is a professional one which is completely different from the emotionally based relationship between parent and child. As soon as the emotional involvement is increased our ability to make objective judgements becomes more difficult. Probably, the most effective way to support and work with parents is to use our professional expertise to consider the developing relationship as a learning process. This learning process can be planned for, reflected on, observed and progress identified. Getting to know parents is an essential part of our work in the same way as getting to know the children. If, as our response to having initial concerns about a child's development, we immediately tell the parents that there is something wrong and that they need to seek professional help, we are likely to get an adverse reaction. However, if we consider our professional understanding of our relationship with the parents, we can focus more effectively on the way in which we can best support these particular parents. Thinking about who is involved in the communication, what information needs to be passed on and when, is crucial to the positive relationship continuing. It may not always be appropriate for the keyworker alone to pass on information, so decisions about when the SENCO, Deputy Manager, etc. needs to be involved should be conscious ones.

Communication about sensitive or emotional issues needs to be considered from the perspective of both the staff and the parent. Thought should be given to:

- who the parents would choose to talk to most if they were concerned
- where this conversation should take place
- when is the best time
- what would need to be included in the discussion.

Considering these at a conscious level enables us to increase the chances of the discussion going well. The pace of the information giving and the evidence base which is contained in the information are the key to parents feeling supported rather than defensive. It is our responsibility to take the lead in finding ways to facilitate the parents' opportunity to access support appropriately. Probably the most challenging situation is where the concerns are focused on the child's behaviour. It is so tempting, after a day when a child has perhaps hit, kicked and bitten, to meet the parents when they come to collect their child with a tirade of the misdemeanours and details of what a bad day you have had. However, our professional role is to share the information in a way which gives a context around the behaviour and indication about what we plan to do to support the child's behavioural learning. Taking this approach enables us to work with parents to consider the possible reasons for this current behaviour and to work together to do some problem solving based on our shared knowledge of the child's understanding and learning.

Throughout this book the importance of a positive relationship with parents is emphasised as central to supporting children's learning and development. This positive relationship does not happen by chance so we need to think consciously about how we can build on and improve our current practice. Given the chance, parents will be able to inform and contribute to this improvement through sharing their experiences of your setting. For this to be effective and useful we need to be careful who we ask and what we ask. It is too easy and not very helpful to ask the parents we like and whom we know will say nice things about us. We need to dig a bit deeper:

- What is it that parents particularly feel was helpful or supportive?

- How can we increase parental involvement in our setting?

- What kind of involvement can we offer to encourage parents to feel they would like to be involved?

- Which parents are least likely to visit our setting? What are we doing to make involvement easier for them?

- What would the parents' priorities be for making our setting more accessible – not just physically but in terms of feeling comfortable, effective communication, information sharing and, of course, attitude?

- What would the parents' priorities be for making our setting more inclusive?

- What can we do to support parents' access to information, training and knowledge about the advantages of an inclusive setting?

The list is endless and, with your parents' help, could be developed as part of your Improvement or Development Plan to drive your journey towards continuous improvement.

**Key points**

- Parents' experiences of understanding and coping with their child's medical needs or diagnosis will vary considerably.

- Even if you initially feel anxious about what adjustments you will make to ensure the child is included, the first welcome for the parent will set the tone of your developing relationship.

- The principles of the Early Support Programme should be guiding our practice in supporting children with disabilities.

- Where possible, bringing together representatives from other involved agencies will reduce misunderstandings and competing priorities. It will also reduce the pressure on parents to be sole co-ordinators of their child's support.

- We need to make conscious decisions about how we will strengthen our relationship with individual parents in order to maximise the opportunities for the child.

- Diagnosis and needs related to behaviour are generally the most challenging in terms of practitioner attitude and supporting parents effectively.

- A positive and supportive relationship with parents can form the basis of involving parents in the continuous improvement of your setting.

| | |
|---|---|
| www.CAF.org.uk | Contact a Family website giving information about various conditions and syndromes with details of support groups for parents |
| www.earlysupport.gor.uk | |
| www.everychildmatters.gov.uk | |
| www.surestart.gov.uk | |
| www.surestart.gov.uk/_doc/p0001372.pdf | Promoting Race Equality in the Early Years |
| www.surestart.gov.uk/publications | Together from the Start |
| www.teachernet.gov.uk/teachingandlearning/ socialandpastoral/sebs1/seal/ | Social Emotional Aspects of Learning |
| www.aimh.org.uk | Association for Mental Health (AIMH) uk |
| www.Itscotland.org.uk/omages/stirling earlyedcasestudy_tcm_161673.pdf | Children as Partners |
| www.coram.org.uk | Coram Family |
| www.daycaretrust.org.uk | Day Care Trust |
| www.earlychildhood.org.uk | |
| www.esmational.org.uk/ec/ecaip.htm | Early Childhood Adventures in Peacemaking |
| www.earlyeducaion.org.uk | Early Education Assocation |
| www.fnn.org.uk | Family Nurturing Network |
| www.incredibleyears.com | Incredible Years (Dina's Dinosaur) |
| www.kidshealth.org | |
| www.ncma.org.uk | National Childminding Association |
| www.nfpi.org.uk | National family & Parenting Institute |
| www.paretnlineplus.org.uk | |
| www.peep.org.uk | |
| www.preschool.org.uk | Preschool Learning Alliance |
| www.rnib.org.uk | Royal National Institute for the Blind |
| www.rnid.org.uk | Royal National Institute for the Deaf |
| www.nspcc.org.uk | National Society for the Prevention of Cruelty to Children |
| www.zerotothree.org | |

The author takes no responsibility for the content of the listed websites but some information may be helpful.

# BIBLIOGRAPHY

Astington, J. W. (1993) *The Child's Discovery of the Mind*. Cambridge, MA: Harvard University Press.

Carlin, J. (2005) *Including Me: Managing Complex Health Needs in Schools and Early Years Settings*. London: Council for Disabled Children/National Children's Bureau.

DfES (2001a) *Ofsted National Standards*. London: Ofsted.

DfES (2001b) *Special Educational Needs Code of Practice*. London: DfES.

DfES (2003) *Every Child Matters*. London: DfES.

DfES (2004) *Removing Barriers to Achievement: The Government's Strategy for SEN*. London: DfES.

DfES (2006) *The Early Years Foundation Stage* (draft). London: DfES.

DfES/QCA (2000) *Curriculum Guidance for the Foundation Stage*. London: QCA.

Disability Rights Commission (2002) *Code of Practice for Schools Disability Discrimination Act 1995*. London: The Stationery Office.

Dowling, M. (2005) *Young Children's Personal, Social and Emotional Development* (second edition). London: Paul Chapman Publishing.

Dunn, J. (2004) *Children's Friendships: The Beginnings of Intimacy*. Oxford: Blackwell Publishing.

Gerhart, S. (2004) *Why Love Matters*. London: Routledge.

Hala, S. (ed.) (1997) *The Development of Social Cognition*. Hove: Psychology Press.

High/Scope (1998) *Supporting Children in Resolving Conflicts* (video).

Karmiloff, K. and Karmiloff-Smith, A. (2001) *Pathways to Language: From Fetus to Adolescent*. Cambridge Mass: Harvard University Press.

Laevers, F. (2000) 'Forward to basics! Deep-level learning and the experiential approach', *Early Years*, 20(2): 20–9.

Pascal, C. (1997) 'The Effective Early Learning Project and the National Curriculum', in T. Cox (ed.) *The National Curriculum and the Early Years: Challenges and Opportunities*. London: Falmer Press.

QCA (2005a) *Seeing Steps in Children's Learning*. London: QCA.

QCA (2005b) *Observing Children – Building the Profile*. London: QCA.

Robinson, M. (2003) *From Birth to One: The Year of Opportunity*. Suffolk: Open University Press.

Sure Start (2002) *Birth to Three Matters: A Framework to Support Children in their Earliest Years*. London: DfES.

Trevarthen, C. (1993) 'The function of emotions in early infant communication and development', in J. Nadel and L. Camaioni (eds) *New Perspectives in Early Communicative Development*. London: Routledge.

Wall, K. (2004) *Autism and Early Years*. London: Paul Chapman Publishing.

Wall, K. (2006) *Special Needs and Early Years* (second edition). London: Paul Chapman Publishing.

# INDEX